T0171070

The  Other F Word

7 DAYS TO FORGIVING ANYONE

JULIANA ERICSON

"*I am not what happened to me. I am what I choose to become.*"

— Carl Jung

BALBOA.
PRESS

A DIVISION OF HAY HOUSE

Balboa Press books may be ordered through booksellers or by contacting:

Balboa Press
A Division of Hay House
1663 Liberty Drive
Bloomington, IN 47403
www.balboapress.com
1-(877) 407-4847

Because of the dynamic nature of the Internet, any web addresses or
links contained in this book may have changed since publication and
may no longer be valid. The views expressed in this work are solely those
of the author and do not necessarily reflect the views of the publisher,
and the publisher hereby disclaims any responsibility for them.

The author of this book does not dispense medical advice or prescribe
the use of any technique as a form of treatment for physical, emotional,
or medical problems without the advice of a physician, either directly
or indirectly. The intent of the author is only to offer information
of a general nature to help you in your quest for emotional and
spiritual well-being. In the event you use any of the information in
this book for yourself, which is your constitutional right, the author
and the publisher assume no responsibility for your actions.

Any people depicted in stock imagery provided by Thinkstock are
models, and such images are being used for illustrative purposes only.
Certain stock imagery © Thinkstock.

Printed in the United States of America.

ISBN: 978-1-4525-7848-4 (sc)
ISBN: 978-1-4525-7849-1 (e)

Balboa Press rev. date: 8/8/2013

Dedication

This book is dedicated to The Holy Spirit,
my teacher, my friend and my guide.

ACKNOWLEDGMENTS

The stories I have written in this book are about many of my clients who had the courage and intention to heal. Without them, there would be no book. They were the inspiration and they were the subjects, although I've changed the names to protect their privacy. It was their courageously changed thinking, their shifts in perception, I compiled for this book. I thank my children, Shannon and Heydn, for supporting me in this work and for being shining examples to the world of what love looks like. I thank my parents for showing me the art of finding silver linings. I thank my teachers, Margo Powell, Debi Miller, Kelly Walden, Sondra Ray, Tony LoMastro, Maureen Malone, Leonard Orr and Patricia Brennan, for teaching me this work and continuing to live out its integrity and message of profound healing. I thank my cat Mozart, who passed on in 2011, for teaching me unconditional love.

I thank Sondra Ray from the bottom of my heart for writing her groundbreaking book "The Only Diet There Is," from which I originally learned the 70 times 7

Forgiveness is the unconditional love of God that we share between people. It is the language of the Divine, the understanding of the heart.
　　　　　　　　　　　　　　　　- Juliana Ericson

TABLE OF CONTENTS

POETRY BY JULIANA ERICSON

Becoming Alive
Good Enough
I Am Willing To Be Willing
Reflections
Worthy
Original Innocence
The Gift
Statement of Truth
Choice Is My Power
The Miracle
I Am Safe
The Truth about Me
Now
Something I Know For Sure
One Precious Thing
Trusting the Flowing Process of Life
Being Peace
Looking For the Good
The Whole World Says Yes To Me
My Love Is Important
With Help, I Can Do It

FORWARD

I believe that real love, not just hearts-and-flowers-love, is the most powerful force in the universe: a force available within every person, which is able to create a bridge from hate to reconciliation. This book is my attempt to show you that this is possible in your life.

- Juliana Ericson, September 1, 2012

"Not forgiving is like drinking rat poison and then waiting for the rat to die."

- Anne Lamott from "Traveling Mercies"

FORGIVENESS

Loosening;
untying;
letting go.

INTRODUCTION

What forgiveness is not: Most people confuse forgiveness with weakness, thinking it's about giving in, or looking the other way when faced with a conflict. That's not forgiveness at all. If we try to achieve peace with those methods, it's likely to come back at us later, disguised as bitterness, loneliness, sickness, or worse. Pushing away a raw, angry feeling, pretending it does not exist, is not peace. That is not healing. Since peace and healing is our desired state, we need to try something different.

It is true that conflict comprises a huge part of life on earth, but we do not have to live with conflict in our own lives. By choosing constructive methods of working with conflict we create a greater opportunity to live in peace. Forgiveness does not justify the wrong, nor does it deny the other person has hurt you. You can forgive the person without excusing the act. Forgiveness elegantly brings a kind of peace that helps you get on with your life.

The process I have written about in this book is really very simple. It involves no one other than you. The only difficult step in the whole process is that you have to choose to do it! *The Other F-Word: 7 Days to Forgiving Anyone* is a compilation of true stories out of hundreds of my clients who have experienced significant and previously unimagined positive changes in their lives with this powerful 7-day process.

> *"I just don't know where I'd be today if I hadn't found this Breathwork and Forgiveness. It has saved my life!"* - Marla, Nashville

> *"My new business venture and new relationship has materialized totally because of my work with you, Juliana. My sessions marked the most profound change I've known in my entire life."* - Mary, Nashville, TN

I have witnessed so many outstanding changes in people's lives! I simply *had* to share the miracles with people like you, who may need one more little nudge to make the final step into the life you want and deserve.

You'll find out how this life-changing process removes the pain, removes the problem and miraculously changes the "facts."

> *"I cannot believe how the universe has turned around and is showing me such love and reflecting such happiness on me since beginning my work with you!"* - Shannon, Nashville teacher

It is common after suffering for years to feel a need to try something different, *anything*, to relieve the emotional pain. We may not even know what "different" would look like. That's the point! We have been angry or blaming so long, we do not know *how* to see things differently. As it says in *A Course in Miracles*, a book I use as a guide in my life, "we must choose to see things differently." And with that choosing we give conscious permission to be changed. We change by taking our lives back when we see we are no longer a victim, no longer powerless in the negative situation.

So, it is at this point we must get some extra support. We ask for help according to our spiritual tradition: Holy Spirit, God, Divine Mother, Krishna, Our Inner Knowing, Great Spirit, . . . In biblical terms they speak of having the faith of a mustard seed and you can do great things. All you have to do is have the willingness of this *i*'s dot, the size of a mustard seed, and God will take care of the "how."

Carolyn Myss teaches, "Say 'yes' not 'how'!" This *yes* we say shouts to the whole universe of our intention. It is from this point that we begin to experience the shift in our perception of the experience which has angered us. Some people see this change as a shift in dimension, which in some ways it is. Things *are* different with that discordant relationship. The way you feel toward the person with whom you were angry *is* changed. Even more remarkable is that the other people do not have to change; they do not even have to know that we are in the process of forgiving them. WE do the changing; we change our minds to see the situation differently.

I hear people defend their anger-thinking with, "I've

tried forgiveness before, and she is still just so hard to get along with!" or "Yes, I've done forgiveness work on my dad. It's just that he'll never change and I've learned to deal with it." These are not reflections of forgiveness; they're "stuffing-it" feelings, "I-don't-want-to-waste-any-more-time-on-him" feelings.

I have been a transformational Life Coach and Breath Teacher for 17 years, helping my clients move through their stuck places and on to happier and more fulfilling lives. Through assisting people in this way I have evolved into what I consider to be a Forgiveness Coach. More often than not people are stuck in blame, not realizing they're holding themselves back and creating their own toxic victim-thinking. That is what's creating the unacceptable lives they resent. It's a vicious cycle; anger can be seductive. Like a gerbil on its wheel, we can choose to step off at any time. We are always at choice.

Do you really want to change?

It takes tremendous courage to choose to be happy and to choose peace. *Notice I wrote "courage," not "difficulty" or "long-suffering."* The courage to which I am referring is the kind that is willing to accept change, to accept being changed, and accept a changed life. You may say you want it, but do you really?

Many people are privately afraid of what change will bring into their lives. *"What will the new me look like, act like, be like? Will I fail at being the new me? Will my friends still want to be with me? Will the unknown be scary? Will my partner accept the changed me?*" Common fears such as these are subconsciously preventing most people from creating the dream lives after which they are endlessly chasing.

In her book "Feel the Fear and Do It Anyway" Susan Jeffers wrote about how even great achievers feel fear. But they do not let fear stop them. They feel it and move forward. I challenge you to feel your fear of forgiving that certain someone in your life, and do it regardless of what fear you may be experiencing. This book will help you in many ways. It will give you real-life examples of others who have felt their fear, moved forward, and experienced peace and joy beyond their wildest imaginings. You can do the same. Take one small step: say yes to letting go. Your willingness is your power.

> "The most significant spiritual growth in my life has happened since I was introduced to Breathwork and you with your Forgiveness teaching."
> - Jim, Nashville singer/songwriter

I know this process works because it works in my own life and in the lives of my clients with whom I have worked. This book contains true stories of people who have forgiven others they once hated, and now live lives full of peace and happiness. If you will commit to complete the small amount of writing required, this Forgiveness Process can also transform your life, in a more gigantic way than you can imagine! I am not making hollow promises here. I am sharing the truth from my own experiences and from those I have personally witnessed through 17 years of my Coaching & Breathwork practice.

Radically different!

There are two approaches to Forgiveness that make this book unusual: First, this Forgiveness process only takes a week to complete. Second, there is the prenatal and birth information I have included in the details of some of the Forgiveness stories. I have been studying since 1996 how our experience in the womb and the circumstances surrounding our birth affect our adult lives, and I am excited to share this valuable information with you. These findings are part of groundbreaking scientific advances in the worlds of prenatal and birth psychologies and psycho-science. One of these sciences is Epigenetics, about which Dr. Bruce Lipton writes in his book *The Biology of Belief.* I have included prenatal and birth psychology information throughout the book, pointing to possible deep-seated reasons for why we are angered at certain people without knowing the reason. This unique book addresses blocks to peace that may exist in our conscious memories, as well as those locked in our subconscious minds. (Concentrated information explaining this unique subject is covered in Chapter 4.)

You will find some action suggestions at the end of each chapter meant to support you in making small steps towards your transformed life. You don't have to know how to change. You merely need to bring your mustard seed of willingness; the rest is Divine Intervention. Relax and enjoy the ride of your life!

BECOMING ALIVE

I have wrongly considered guilt and blame
*   to be my friends and protectors.*
We would have long conversations
about what wrongs had been done to me in such great detail.
The more I would talk about my past hurts
*   with my friends, Guilt and Blame,*
the larger the hurt became and the darker my vision became.
These conversations about my story
*   made me bitter and resentful,*
*   angry at the other, but angrier at myself.*
I realize Guilt and Blame are not my friends at all.
They have prevented me from joining life.
Today I choose to divorce guilt and blame from my mind
*   and begin to replace them with forgiveness,*
*   beginning with myself.*
This is a good day
*   because I am reborn to the living.*

– Juliana Ericson

"If anyone has a complaint against another, forgive each other, just as the Lord has forgiven you, so you must also forgive."
-Colossians 3:13
(*English Standard Version*)

CHAPTER 1

Benefits of Thinking Like a Cat

Here is my cat, Mozart, sitting next to me as I am writing this book. He has been one of my greatest teachers: of patience, of gratitude, of being present, of unconditional love, even of forgiveness. Many people's version of forgiveness is about judging others as wrong or bad. Many, even deeply spiritual people, see forgiveness as a bitter pill to swallow, or maybe a giant monster they must stuff into a little box within themselves. Sometimes people think forgiving a wrongdoer would be even worse than holding a gun to your head, then pulling the trigger!

So how does my cat fit into all of this? He shows me how upside-down my thinking really is. Mozart's view of Forgiveness is not to judge in the first place. His perspective is more like what I think God's view is: Forgiveness is not necessary, because He does not judge that we have done anything wrong. God sees us perfect, whole and complete, as we were created to be and still are. Our Divine Creator sees ONLY what HE made in us, which has never changed. We see only what WE HAVE made. Therein lies the problem.

This may sound all sweet and fuzzy. It works in movies and fiction, but how can you use this type of thinking in the "real" world? By willing to be happy, I mean really ready and willing to be happy. You may think you are ready for a new life and are praying for relief of a problem, praying for the person to change or for things to be different. However, these things cannot happen until you let go of the poison, so to speak.

A new life emerges when we let go of our old way of thinking. This is such a simple concept, but we make it so complicated. It's like trying to pour fine, aged wine into a glass full of polluted water. Yuck! Instead, we should pour out and clean the glass of the toxins, *then* pour in the fine wine. This comparison is similar to how we deal with problems. We have polluted our lives with bitterness, anger, revenge, fear and so on. No wonder the dream lives do not materialize. We are trying to create something wonderful in the midst of a toxic-waste dump. It cannot happen. (Well, maybe it *can* happen, in extreme circumstances, but generally it does not.) The best part of this little story is, you do not have to wait a lifetime to clean up your private toxic dump, nor does it have to be difficult and painful. It merely takes the willingness of that teeny-tiny mustard seed, capable of moving mountains. That is what this book is about. It is a compilation of real stories about real people moving mountains. Read on and be amazed!

> "He who would not forgive must judge, for he must
> justify his failure to forgive."
> > - A Course in Miracles, W401

What a powerful realization it was for me to really understand this statement above! Guilt will demand punishment from whomever or whatever it can find. We may want to say: "It's NOT my fault, it's his!" or "Don't you know what she did to me?!" We want it to be *them* who is guilty. We do not want to blame ourselves for the pain we are feeling, or the wrong we may have done. We want to get rid of the painful guilt we are feeling. We will project that guilt onto others while we stay resentful, angry and bitter, sometimes for years. All too often, we don't want to forgive the person we are angry with; if we did, then *who would we blame for how badly we feel?* We think we need a scapegoat, a whipping post, a dumping ground for our pain.

Why forgive? Why not just forget?

> "I had no idea that this Forgiveness Process would
> be this powerful! I thought I had moved through
> that stuff years ago with all the work I've done
> over the years."
> > - Nancy, Massage Therapy trainer

When we say we have forgotten an issue that once angered us, what that often means is that we have merely stuffed the memory. We still carry around the emotional implications of an emotional trauma, years after it has occurred. We continue to carry the anger in the cells of our body. You could say we can continue to experience that trauma—emotionally, mentally and physically at a cellular level—until it is released. Experiences that created a negative response in us when we were young get carried through to our later years and can condense in our bodies as *dis-eases*, if they are left without attention. These emotional challenges can solidify in our emotional bodies to become feelings: bitterness, anger and depression. Within our mental bodies, pessimism, negativism and blame can result from those stuffed painful emotions we carry around for years.

It's not only that the emotional trauma stored in our cells actually gets stuck and hardens there. It multiplies. As The Law of Attraction states, we draw to ourselves what we believe. Those stuffed subconscious thoughts and feelings draw to themselves just as much life experience as the conscious ones. If we have a core negative thought that life is a struggle, then we will draw to us experiences proving that is true. I have learned that about 85 percent of our thoughts are subconscious. Much of that is our bodies' functioning capabilities. Some of it, though, is comprised of our stuffed thoughts, judgments, fears and pre-verbal programming. This negative concoction of subconscious thoughts is what may cause us the most harm. If we are unaware of those thoughts, they can be pretty damaging.

When we say, "*I've forgotten about that; it's in the past!*"

that is another way of saying, "*I've stuffed it, and I don't want to think about it right now. I feel safer with it stored in a very deep place behind really thick armor!*" We believe it will not hurt us if we do not think about it, but that's just not true. We do hurt ourselves by stuffing those toxic emotions and often, we also hurt others.

So let's look at our subconscious a little more closely.

Our thoughts can make us sick

Researcher Dr. Bruce Lipton wrote, "The New Biology will take you from a world of crisis and ill health to another level of masterful control. Epigenetic control equals control over your genes. If you're controlled by your genes, you're a victim of your genes. But, it is your mind that controls your genes, your genetic expression." With regard to cancer and the new science of Epigenetics, Dr. Lipton explains, "As it turns out, your genetic blueprint is not the problem. There is no cancer gene. The source of the problem is the readout of the blueprint: how your cells interpret the directions from your mind."

Isn't that amazing? In other words, our beliefs can change our genetic expression! We are in charge of our health in a way most of us have never realized. Our beliefs can make us sick, but our beliefs can also heal us. We are in charge of them, at least the ones we're aware of in that conscious 15 percent area. I want to show you in this book how you can learn what unhealthy thoughts might be lurking in that other 85 percent, your subconscious, and clean them out.

We are also influenced by the beliefs of those around us; they affect our energy field. If our culture, family, and friends do not believe we can heal, that influences our ability to do so. Beliefs are energy fields that shape our genetic expression. Dr. Lipton talks about Jesus not being able to heal others in his own hometown. That might have been because people in his town had known him from the time he was a boy, and did not believe he could heal the sick. Jesus said you can renew your life through your beliefs. Epigenetics shows this is true.

The placebo effect is an example of how positive beliefs can make you better. *Nocebos* are negative beliefs; they can make you sick, or even kill you.

> *"The new science has EVERTHING to do with your beliefs!"* - Dr. Bruce Lipton

This leads me to the reason I decided to write this book in the first place. When we choose to be angry, resentful or hateful, we choose to stuff our feelings. We also choose the negative energy field that goes with those feelings, allowing that to abide in our body. This negative energy field is what I believe Eckhart Tolle is referring to when he talks about "the pain body," as a collection of negative energies we have created and choose to carry with us (as judgments, anger, resentment, bitterness and so on). These energies may be directed at ourselves, or at others. Either way they are hurting our potential to enjoy a full life of love and purpose. Meanwhile, as Dr. Lipton has proven, these energies can also make us sick.

You are safe. You are innocent. You are loved.

What if these words were really true? What if you have been living your whole life denying your magnificence, not realizing you are already worthy? Who would you be if you really knew you are worthy now? You do not even have to try to be loved, because you already are completely and unconditionally loved. Imagine the fabulous relationships you could have if you did not have to judge or hurt others in defense, because you understood you were already innocent!

ACTION: Think of a recurring or constant pain you are experiencing. What was going on in your life when it first occurred? A crisis? A disappointment? Are there any connections between when your pain started and a negative situation or a person involved in or during that situation? What decision did you make about that person?

You are safe. You are innocent. You are loved.

"Good Enough" by Juliana Ericson
www.JulianaNashville.com

GOOD ENOUGH

I know that I am good enough.
I have spent way too many years wasting time
trying to prove this truth to myself,
    to people in my life
        even trying to prove it to strangers.
Today is the day I will stop this madness.
I am good enough.
    I am good enough.
        I am good enough.
To the entire world and to myself I proclaim:
"I am good enough!"

– Juliana Ericson

"To forgive is to set a prisoner free and discover that the prisoner was you."

- Lewis B. Smedes

CHAPTER 2

Consider Forgiving Yourself First

I suggest that you forgive yourself before forgiving others. I recommend this because once you experience how far-reaching this transformation is, it will be easier for you to be inspired to complete the process on others who are stumbling blocks to your peace. After you have seen the power of this Forgiveness Process you may use it like a magic eraser in your consciousness to remove other toxic residue and emotional gunk. Let it go!

It is when I saw huge shifts in life after completing my first Forgiveness Process that I began believing change was actually possible. Radically different change: the kind where you feel your innocence again; where you feel like you *can* become brand new, and begin again. It's a change that wipes away all the bad you thought you were, and that you thought others were. I had never felt that type of change before. I was used to pretending, or giving in to others, the way I had been taught in my family. I was used to looking the other way, stuffing it, taking the abuse or giving it to myself. But change, innocence and beginning anew? No, these concepts were not even on my radar screen. I understand neither the language nor the reasoning. I was only used to guilt, blame and suffering.

My own story

I will now share my own forgiveness-story so you will understand what I mean. I was widowed from a wonderful man at the age of 37. My two-year-old son and I were left with a secure amount of money. I was lonely for the first couple of years, and then met Tom. He was handsome, charming, fun, brilliant and sexy, and he knew exactly what to say to melt my heart. He started a company that provided nursing/medical care for very sick children in their homes. *"Awwwh! What a sweet, guy!"* I thought. I was hooked.

Not long into our relationship, Tom's company began running into financial troubles. He told me that he had squeezed every dime he could to no avail, and that he needed money that week for payroll or he'd have to close the business. He asked me for a loan of $20,000. Tom promised that his company was just going through a rough spot, and would be back on its feet in no time. He smiled that big, gorgeous smile and made me feel safe and comfortable enough to write him a check, which I did.

The next week I co-signed a $50,000 loan for Tom's business. That financial drain kept going on for many months, and it ended up being more than just for his business loans. I finished paying for his doctorate degree in Economics at Vanderbilt, paid his monthly Porsche payments, wrote more checks, more, more, more. . . .

I discovered a few months into our two-year relationship that Tom really liked women—lots of women. What made matters worse was, it turned out some of the money I was giving him was being used to take these other women on romantic trips and out to expensive dinners. In fact it was one of those nights when a waiter who knew me and was working at a pricey restaurant called to ask if I had given Tom my credit card to take this lovely lady to dinner. I dropped everything, drove like a crazy woman over to the restaurant, saw Tom with his latest conquest and ended it with him right there.

After all was said and done, I had loaned him almost a quarter of a million dollars. Near the beginning I had prepared a loan agreement, which we both had signed. After it was too late I found that he had gone through my files and destroyed it. I tried to sue him, but he said I had given him all that money as a gift, not expecting repayment. I had no proof that the money had only been loaned.

A month into the lawsuit, Tom died of a heart attack. I never did get my money back. The IRS was ahead of me on the repayment list, if any money had ever been found. I had to eat the loss. I sold my beautiful dream home to recoup some of the money. Then my daughter left me during the fiasco, hating to see me abuse myself so badly in that toxic relationship (more on that later). I went through a major depression for about 6 months. It was really awful. Meanwhile, my young son had to deal with it, not knowing what to do to help me.

I had focused all my time on Tom for those two years, letting my friends and my church family go, so now no one even came to visit me. It was a pitiful time, probably the lowest in my life. Fortunately, I found Breathwork, *A Course in Miracles* and meditation, all within a couple of months of each other. Together they pulled me out of my incredibly deep hole and pointed me in the direction of the empowered woman I have become today.

It was the Forgiveness Process in my Breathwork sessions that dynamited me into a whole new place. I have to admit that I did *not* want to forgive Tom. I really hated him at that point, for how he had stolen my happiness from me. I felt he had stolen my future, my home, my daughter, my self-esteem. I blamed him for it all!

There's a lesson in *A Course in Miracles* that says "I'm willing to see things differently." Somewhere deep inside, I knew that was the truth. I had to see things differently, because I needed to become alive again. I wanted to be part of my son's life! I wanted more than just feeling like stone, more than feeling bitter, angry and resentful. I knew there *had* to be another way.

So I began the Forgiveness Process, focused on forgiving Tom. I cried during the whole thing. I cried as I wrote each word; I cried for me and I cried for my children. I cried for what I had lost, and for what I would never have. I let myself mourn one last time.

By the end of the week I was feeling lighter, like my feet

were walking just above the ground, and I couldn't even feel it. My heart had a lightness I had not experienced in years. I began smiling for no reason. The lump in my throat that had been ever-present, holding back constant sadness for so long, was gone. It was like a veil had been pulled back between me and the people around me. I was reborn.

Once I got to that point, I knew there was more work for me to do. Now I could accomplish more positive changes, because I had the strength; I was refueled. I then went on to do a Forgiveness Process on myself. After I had forgiven Tom, I could see a whole layer of disgust and self-hate that I needed to heal inside of me. I dove in.

Since the process of forgiveness is to let go, we are the ones who need to do the letting go. I have found that it helps to create a clean slate within ourselves before we begin the Forgiveness Process on others. It is harder to do this work on other people when we still have buried anger directed at ourselves.

> *"Faith is taking the first step even when you can't see the whole staircase."*
>
> - Martin Luther King, Jr.

Sarah's stuff

Sarah seemed to have it all: She was a successful engineer, funny and beautiful. She was living the good life, with an expansive weekend home on the lake, a super nice speedboat, a new Mercedes Benz, frequent vacations and a fabulous condo. As Sarah spoke in her session with me, however, she began to cry, explaining that she was over her head in debt. She was having trouble sleeping and developing stomach problems from the stress of bill collectors' constant calls, asking about her late payments. Although she had come to me because of her poor relationship with her mother, her financial mess was what came up for her to be healed first.

She was making a great income but only had debt to show for it. Each month she had had to charge more and more essentials on her credit cards just to live. Sarah was angry at herself for letting her finances become so desperate. She knew she had to let go of her expensive Mercedes payments, but was too embarrassed to let the beautiful car go. What would her friends think? How could she face them? The Benz represented success to her and if she sold it for another car she would feel a failure, and she thought her friends would agree. She did not think she could stand the embarrassment.

Although it had originally been intended to please and impress her hyper-critical mother, Sarah had to realize that her overspending was ultimately her own personal failing. She finally got to the point of accepting responsibility, stopped blaming her mother and was ready to do the Forgiveness Process on herself, in hope of stopping her financial hemorrhaging.

Sarah was not even finished with the seven days of writing in her Forgiveness Process before she attracted a perfect solution to her Mercedes problem. A friend was moving back to Montana and needed to sell her trendy, gently-used Land Rover. Done! Sarah scarfed it up for $1,200, sold her Mercedes and paid her credit-card bill down. Win/win! No more $500 monthly car payments, *and* she now got to drive a car that better fit her outdoorsy personality.

The next week she found a condo in the same complex, with only two bedrooms instead of the four-bedroom unit she was living in, and at half the price. The next month she sold her vacation home and paid off her debt in full. Her stomach problems went away and she began sleeping restfully again. Sarah had forgiven herself and learned that the letting-go process of Forgiveness is pure freedom: freedom from guilt, freedom from debt, freedom from stuff, and freedom from blame.

> *"Perhaps the greatest impact from my Forgiveness Process came when I realized I "liked" the strokes I got from being a widow. I have no doubt that my personal tragedies were playing a key role in my daily life, and that I actually drew strength from people "stroking" me as the poor little victim of rotten circumstances. I am not doing that anymore. I realize that I don't need that kind of strength. I need to forgive myself and move forward instead, empowering myself through this exciting opportunity to create my future on a relatively blank canvas."* - Mary

Set yourself free

Carol had been a mistake. Her parents had not wanted to be pregnant at 17, and everyone in the family had agreed that her mother having a child at that time was not a good thing. Carol had not been wanted by anyone. The anger in her family had continued through the entire pregnancy, creating what we call an "emotionally toxic" womb.

This environment creates a "world" for the growing child who does not feel safe, which often creates anxiety and depression in adulthood. It is common for people with this beginning to believe the world is not welcoming, and they may choose to separate themselves from social involvements. People with this origin can benefit greatly from learning they have the power to change positively, using such healing processes as the prenatal psychology work I write about in this book.

Carol had spent her entire life feeling inadequate, a burden, unworthy and unwanted. She'd felt as though her presence on this planet was a waste of space. She'd allowed herself to be mistreated by men, including her former husband. She had worked at the same job for 32 years, which she absolutely hated, only because she'd been sure no one else would hire her, so why even try.

You can probably guess her response when I asked if she was willing to forgive herself for not recognizing her own worthiness. Carol's eyes bugged out of her head and her meek voice let out a squeal. "Oh no, I couldn't do that!" Her unworthiness would not allow her to even say the words, "I forgive myself for not being kind to myself." or "I forgive myself for allowing myself to be devalued by men." I explained that the more resistant she was to this potential positive change, the greater the gift would be when she let it go. Her birthday was coming up, and she was intrigued by the gift idea, so she started. She emailed me three times to get support while writing the first part of the process; her mind just would not settle down long enough to concentrate.

After completing the Forgiveness Process, Carol saw her new boyfriend turn a corner when he paid for them both to spend her upcoming birthday weekend at a lovely beach house. Up until then, he had usually had her pay her own expenses, and had never offered a gift such as this. He was being unusually kind and thoughtful. In addition, she received dozens of phone calls from friends and family on her birthday, making her feel newly wanted and loved. Forgiveness was a great birthday gift to herself! She felt the gift of being wanted, of being worthy and being loved.

ACTION: Think of a person who makes you feel like a victim, whether or not it was intentional. How does your feeling toward that person feel in your body? Do your muscles tense up? Do you get a knot in your stomach, or clench your teeth? Just notice . . . .

You are safe. You are innocent. You are loved.

by Nila Frederiksen

I Am Willing To Be Willing

Just like cleaning out an old closet in my basement,
I want to clear out my subconscious
     of all the unresolved blame and anger
          I feel toward others.
I have stuffed these old issues into a dark room,
     locking them away,
               assuming no one would know about them.
I now realize that these old, dusty issues never go away,
     they only grow in intensity.
They are constantly growing and alive, wanting to be released.
I am ready to do that now.
I am ready to begin the clearing out of dust and cobwebs.
I will begin releasing these issues today,
          knowing I am doing it for my own best interest,
               doing it for my larger life yet to be lived.

– Juliana Ericson

"Forgiveness is not something you do for someone else; it's something you do for yourself."   - Jim Beaver

CHAPTER 3

Drop the Rope

The original Greek translation of forgiveness was "to loosen" or "to untie." It did not mean "*They were right; I am wrong. I'm a loser to forgive them.*" It has nothing to do with our version of surrender, nor does it have anything to do with being right or wrong. It has everything to do with being happy and really letting go, letting go of what has been holding us back from experiencing the fulfilling life we say we want.

I have known folks who have remained angry with people who have passed on. Think about that for a minute. If the person with whom you're mad is dead, and you're still angry, just *who* are you arguing with? You are arguing with yourself! Such a waste of time and joy. You're arguing with a dead person's memory inside your head, and you are miserable! So who is winning here?

There is a great Buddhist lesson I like to pass on to my clients. The gist of it is that there are two people playing tug-of-war, each pulling on their own end of the rope. Back, forth, back, forth. Harder, back, harder, forth they pull. What happens when one drops the rope? There is no more game; it takes two. It's the same with arguing: When one person lets go, or forgives, even if the fight has lasted a lifetime, there is no more argument. It takes two to have an argument. That doesn't mean we are saying the other person is right and we are wrong. It just means we have dropped or untied the rope, just as Jesus meant when he used the term forgiveness 2,000 years ago.

At first, the concept of not having anger with someone who has wronged us can make us feel defenseless. We may feel vulnerable because we are used to having a defense-shield up against that person (or even against anyone who acts or looks like that person). Some defense-shields are created as extra body weight. Some are emotional sheets of armor that repel others, while making the defensive person feel alone and lonely. Yet other defense shields materialize as over-busyness or over-being-needed. Sometimes they appear as control and manipulation, or even "over-niceness" (a kind of pretending that's emotionally and physically draining to continue for long). Whatever the defense we have used, it's time to let it go, time to be happy. It's time to live the full lives we deserve to have, that are exciting, fulfilling and worth living!

The real freedom

Although some situations may be awful or even horrendous, this forgiveness is still possible. I once read a story about Amish mothers in Pennsylvania and how they dealt with their children being murdered. A deranged man had burst into the schoolroom of those defenseless children and massacred them. It is beyond all of my mental capabilities to imagine what that community and those parents had to endure! I shudder to think of it now.

Even though those pacifists did not understand the hate and violence inside the killer, they did know one thing. They knew that if they did not forgive him they would be in their own type of hell, and they did not want any part of that. They knew they had no control over what had happened to their children, but they could control their response to the situation. The mothers would not feel helpless; they decided that no matter how horrible the situation, forgiveness was their only way out. (The full story of these courageous people is in the documentary "Forgiveness.")

With forgiving, layers of pain, resentment, guilt and anger are dislodged and then transformed into healthy emotions. Forgiveness has great psychological benefits in purging these poisonous emotions from our bodies. Left unresolved, past hurts can contribute to depression and anxiety, undermining the immune system as well as opening possibilities for creating many otherwise preventable diseases. I feel the worst pain being unforgiving can cause is that it keeps us from experiencing real freedom: freedom from the bonds we think others are holding around us, while *we* are the ones holding the key to those bonds. We have the choice to stay in the struggle or live in freedom. With our freedom of choice we can choose heaven or hell in any moment; *yes we can*!

> *"I am so full of joy right now! My older sister called me and this was the LAST THING I thought she would say: 'Do you remember when you wrote me about forgiving that guy who raped me? Remember how upset I got with you, because I thought I had already forgiven him? He kept popping up in my head and I even dreamed about him. Well, just the other day I ran into him downtown. I hadn't seen him in over 8 years!! All the hate came back to me and I realized that I truly hadn't forgiven him.... I just wanted to tell you that I'm doing the Forgiveness Process and thank you!'"* - Kara

> *"I never thought I was the source of all my problems to begin with—I was ready to hear that I just needed a little fine tuning, and the feeling of being stuck would go away. I would be able to move on, 'full steam ahead' with my desires.*

> *"This is the part where I laugh, because after six Breathwork sessions, I can look back and say,'God has a way of showing you where you are in life by what is IN your life.'*

> *"Breathing is part two of a healing session, and it can only be described as AMAZING. If you have*

to feel to heal, then breathing is the catalyst to forgiveness, letting go and infusing you with love like you've never felt before. It helps you love, to love YOU and everyone around you. Even when you THINK you're happy, this Breathwork takes it to a new level.

"For me, negative thoughts are instantly released, and positive ones are reinforced. It really is GENTLE and POWERFUL at the same time … it's like a washing machine that gets rid of dirt … but some of those 'stains' have been untreated for so long, that they need a few more treatments before they become clean.

"I appreciate Juliana so much for guiding me through this process and being part of my healing journey." ‑ Marika

ACTION: Think of the person in your whole, entire life with whom you are angriest. Close your eyes, take a deep breath. Try to sense in your body all the chains of anger that are connected to that person. Think of all the times this anger has prevented you from feeling joy. Try to feel a tiny mustard seed of willingness to be happy now. Pray that your mustard seed will be nourished as you read this book.

You are safe. You are innocent. You are loved.

"I Did It!" by Juliana Ericson
www.JulianaNashville.com

Reflections

Today
I will attempt to see the good in everyone I encounter.
I will remember
that they, too, were created in God's image
and have divinity within them.
I will try my best to sense that truth
in each and every person I see today.

– Juliana Ericson

> *"I marinated in a toxic womb. I took on all of my mother's stuff!"* - Ilanya Vanzant

CHAPTER 4

Womb & Birth Experiences Well Worth Investigating

Most people have no idea how much their birth and womb experience affects their adult lives. People cannot understand how their premature birth, followed by four weeks in an incubator, might have created an intimacy crisis in their adult lives that they cannot seem to overcome. Most people would think their cesarean-section entries into this world have nothing to do with their inability to complete projects easily or really feel safe. When people are angered without knowing why, the origin might be hidden in their subconscious minds. One person might be fighting with her mate, when subconsciously she is angry with her father because he was verbally abusive to her mother during the womb experience. Perhaps another person who had forceps used at birth cannot hold down a job because of consistent anger at his bosses (which is common for forceps-birthed people).

A simple explanation

What happened at your birth and during your prenatal experience has much to do with who you are today. It begins with what was going on in your parents' lives when you were in the womb. I am not a scientist, so I can only explain it the way I understand it. You probably know that whatever your mother ate, drank or smoked went through her body's bloodstream, through the placenta and into you as a developing fetus. So in essence you ate, drank and smoked whatever she did.

It also works with the chemicals that were circulating in the hormones throughout your mother's body. When your parents hugged or your father touched your mom's body, the neurotransmitter oxytocin circulated through her and through you (By the way, oxytocin is released in large amounts during labor, during the distention of the cervix.) On the opposite side of the spectrum, when she was anxious or frightened, the stress-hormone cortisol was transmitted through your bloodstream as it was going through hers. Whatever she experienced in her life before you were born, you experienced.

We are walking drugstores, and have countless chemicals coursing through our veins daily. It's the way our body communicates in order to function. The problem comes when we have a build-up of one of these chemicals, such as the powerful stress-hormone cortisol. Cortisol is for emergency responses and is intended to help you fight off threats, as it did in primordial times in assisting our ancestors ward off threats from predators and other conflict. It's not meant to be produced in large amounts on a daily basis. When a pregnant woman is under stress or anger on a sustained basis, she is sending this cortisol to her developing fetus on a regular basis, teaching the fetus that life is not safe and that it's a scary place. That early belief, based on the experiences of the mother, becomes part of the emotional fabric of that growing child. Later it often becomes a core belief in the adult mind.

Healing begins with recognition

You can investigate some of your own subconsciously programmed patterns from your prenatal experience right now:

- *Did your parents fight a lot when you were a young child or a developing fetus?* If yes, it could have taught you that relationships are unsupportive, unsafe or even violent. It's probable that you cannot imagine having a peaceful relationship. Do you feel more "at home" with dissension, maybe even picking fights with peaceful people to create the dissension you expect and crave to feel normal?

- *Was your father present during your mother's pregnancy?* If not, your thought could now be "men I love aren't there for me." Maybe you create mates who are not emotionally available to you, or have jobs out of town.

- *Did your father have an affair during the pregnancy?* If yes, you might now believe that loving partners are bound to be unfaithful. Or maybe you are overly jealous of your mate, expecting him/her to cheat (whether they will or not). It is usually difficult for you to trust and feel safe in relationships.

- *Was there a miscarriage within months of your parents becoming pregnant with you?* The womb takes on a type of sadness after a miscarriage, still-birth or abortion. Children born into these wombs tend to have a melancholy that is unexplained by conventional therapy. It can sometimes even create an unexplained depression through their whole lives.

These are a few examples of what a womb experience can do to affect an adult life. Because all healing begins with recognition, I believe that most conditions can be helped with conscious reprogramming, using far-reaching prenatal psychology work such as mine, combined with Conscious Breathwork and Forgiveness.

Her depression began in the womb

I had a session with a young woman who was five months pregnant. Carla came to me because she was depressed, anxious and constantly nauseated. She said she has suffered from mild depression most of her life, but it had become more severe since she had become pregnant. I asked her questions about her own womb and birth experience, and learned that her mother had miscarried twice before being pregnant with her. Both of Carla's parents had been extremely anxious about the pregnancy, working hard to make sure this first child would be born healthy. The last few months her mother had been put on bed rest, and been almost inconsolable about not wanting to hurt her baby. After Carla's birth her mother had suffered from *post-partum* depression and had again had to stay in bed for weeks.

As I have explained earlier, what our mothers experience during our pregnancy, we experience. Her mother had experienced fear and anxiety during the pregnancy. Carla had developed in a womb where two embryos had died before her. I believe that her fear, anxiety and depression may have originated from these causes. I even have proof that my hunch was correct. Carla called me after she returned home the evening of her first Breath Session, telling me she had just finished eating a delicious dinner her loving husband had prepared for her. That was the first meal she had been able to keep down for weeks. In the months after her child was born, she thanked me for helping her see the pattern she had carried for so long. She had located it and transformed it with conscious breathing, spearheaded by her willingness to change.

Our birth experience and our adult patterns

Birth is a dynamic explosion of life, powerfully moving from one experience to another in a matter of hours or minutes. We go from living in a liquid environment to breathing air. For nine months we have lived in a dark, intimate, nurturing home, where the sound of our mother's body was all we heard. Then in an instant we are barraged with bright lights, loud noises and separation from our mothers, as they take us to be cleaned up in the cold room by strangers. In most cases birth in our modern world has outgrown the beautiful and sacred experience it once was. Now it's more like a business, having to do with schedules, profits and insurance costs, rather than allowing the beauty of life to amaze us with Her power and mystery.

I have witnessed hundreds of Breathwork sessions over the past seventeen years and have repeatedly seen how deep-seated emotional blocks can be moved or undone with this work involving prenatal and birth psychology. Although there are many birth types with many more expressions of those patterns, I will write about a few of the most common ones here. I want to give you an idea of how deep and profound this programming is in our bodies. Examples that follow will show how that 85 percent of our mind, our subconscious, holds the keys to our peace and freedom.

Abandonment issues can begin in the womb

People whose fathers deserted their mothers while pregnant can set up an abandonment pattern so that, as adults, they attract mates into their lives who are destined to leave them. For instance, a client I had just last week had created this pattern *in utero*: Her father had left her mother when her mother was seven months pregnant. My client's pattern has been to get angry or antsy after seven months (or seven years) into her love relationships. She is now in the seventh year of her marriage and has been literally pushing her husband away with angry words that seem to fly out of her mouth. "*I can't seem to stop myself! I don't know why I say those mean things to him.*"

The good news is that healing begins with recognition. My client can now rebuild her beliefs about what intimacy should be, safe and nurturing, after letting go of her anger-energy. Currently that anger is keeping her stuck in the past pain her mother had felt many years ago. Introducing her to this Forgiveness Process allows her to forgive her father for leaving her pregnant mother and begin reprogramming her own beliefs about what a committed love relationship can be for her.

Induced births

These people tend to have the underlying thought "How dare you!" and often have irritability they cannot manage or understand. They hate being controlled or manipulated by others. These people were born under someone else's timetable and were not "ready" to be born. Nature has a process that is perfect and wise. Would you tell an oak tree how to grow from an acorn to a hundred-foot, mature tree? An acorn knows what to do. There is a life-force in charge that is all-knowing and powerful.

It's the same with birth: When a child is induced to be born, instead of allowing it to be born when the child is ready, inducing becomes a way of forcing nature to do something unnatural. Induced births tend to create people who have to be induced to do things, and then resent the induction. Sometimes they feel the need to get even by withholding themselves from people and situations.

By the way, I once learned at a Nursing Midwife conference that inducing only works 50 percent of the time, so the question might be, why do it at all!

Cesarean section births and separation

A common trait among people who were born by cesarean section is their difficulty in completing tasks. Birth was not "finished," so to speak, and therefore they were not programmed to finish things. We begin learning about life before we are in school, before we are toddlers, before we are babies. We begin learning about life at birth, and before.

Cesarean-section people often feel helpless. This comes from the fact that a cesarean-section birth is really surgery. These births take place in a surgical room with white masks, cold temperatures, beeping machines, bright lights, lots of knives and blood. When mothers are drugged for the surgery, so are the babies. Nothing is nurturing about a C-section, for sure!

With this birth type some other characteristics emerge: These people can be easily confused because of the anesthesia they received at birth through their mothers; they resent others manipulating them (as the OB/GYN manipulated them, cheating them of their natural birth process); they easily get lost (they were born from a unfamiliar place, and were thus "lost"). They also generally fear completion, because completion represents the end of their nine months: birth. Since their birth was so traumatic, completion can represent death to them, so they often survive by remaining incomplete.

Separation of newborn baby and mother

The final characteristic I will speak about concerning a cesarean-section birth has to do with the necessary separation that takes place. When the mother gives birth using this method and is under anesthesia, the medical team must take the child away from the mother, because she is usually unconscious. *The moment of mother meeting child and child meeting mother is one of the most important moments of a person's life.* When this bonding is not allowed to happen there is a disconnect in the child's brain-to-body communication.

This problem is further exacerbated when the child is brought to the nursery, for hours or even days. Separation of babies from mothers also takes place with other types of birth (premature, post-epidural, forceps-using or other trauma experienced at time of birth). The terror these newborn babies experience, due to separation from their mothers, is beyond comprehension. Traits which show up later in life as a result of these occurrences include apathy, co-dependency, separation anxiety, fear of intimacy and fear of life itself. Common thoughts adults with these traumatic birth experiences incorporate into their psyches are: *They don't want me. I can't get what I want. I must have done something wrong. I am terrified. I have to be alone to survive…* Take a breath!

Long labor

People born with a long labor for their birth experience usually take longer to do things than others do. Do not bother trying to rush them along, because they do not like to be rushed and will rebel. I was in labor for nineteen hours with my son. He takes *forever* to do things as an adult. Some born with a long labor may experience thoughts like "*Life is a struggle!*" or "*I can't do it right!*" because of how long it took for them to be born.

Wrong sex

If a person was born as a girl but one of the parents wanted a boy, or vice versa, that person may have the thought, "I am wrong" or "I am a disappointment" or "I'm not good enough." These people can feel unaccepted, resentful in relationships or maybe just dissatisfied with life. They often see the world as an unfriendly place because they don't feel valued. We are pure love. As babies we are loving and joyous creatures. When we are not met with the same value and joy at birth or in the womb, we emotionally cringe, assuming the problem is us: that we have done something wrong or there is something wrong with us.

Unplanned pregnancy and not being wanted

Even if the parents want to get pregnant, sometimes the timing is just too difficult to have a child: mothers finishing college degrees; three small children and unable to care for any more; father just lost his job; family moving to another city; etc. All of these stresses are enough to handle without having to also deal with being pregnant. All the while the child feels the anxiety going on in its outer environment. Children become programmed with *I'm not wanted* or *I'm a burden*, which follows them through life. It is common for them to be addicted to rejection in relationships; or, conversely, they make themselves indispensable so they won't be rejected. Very often they feel very insecure and vulnerable in relationships.

We teach people how to treat us based on our thoughts about ourselves.

We carry pre-verbal thoughts through to adulthood

An example I often give students to describe this concept is: A seventeen-year-old couple is in high school and find out they are pregnant. The young mother thinks "Oh no! I *can't* be pregnant! I'm still in school; I have my whole life ahead of me. What am I going to do?!" The growing child inside her senses all of this and zeroes in on the thought/feeling her mother had. The baby translates it to "I'm not wanted."

In time, even though the couple may get married and lovingly raise the little girl, she still feels that she is unwanted. A few years later, when kids are playing in the yard, picking teams for soccer, she is not chosen. We always subconsciously teach people how to treat us, so they can live in the reality with us that we have created for ourselves. The little girl believes she was not wanted, so she has taught the children what she believes about herself. They did not choose her, so her thought "I'm not wanted" is affirmed.

As she grows older, she becomes promiscuous. She feels she has to be overtly sexual to get boys to like her, believing otherwise she is unwanted. She also hangs out with a group of teens considered outcasts by the rest. They all hold the belief "I'm not wanted." In her adult years, she never seems able to find a man who will stay, or even treat her with love. It's difficult for her to find a loving relationship when her subconscious is constantly sending out signals to the contrary.

People who were unplanned or not wanted often feel rejected, or will reject others. They want to reject them before they are inevitably rejected. It's also common for them to over-please; they want to be wanted so much, they bend over backward to feel needed or wanted. Planning can often be troublesome for these unplanned people.

Forceps

First and foremost, forceps birth is about authority and anger issues. Our OB/GYN was our first authority figure, the one who manipulated us without our permission. If that manipulation was easy and nurturing, there is usually no residual emotional problem to deal with. But if the delivery team caused pain or suffering, to either baby or mother, whether intentional or not, there is a strong tendency for those people to grow up resenting authority. They do not feel safe. (I always recommend that these people do a Forgiveness Process on their OB/GYN for this reason. It's amazing how Forgiving an unknown person, in this case a doctor, can create such a dramatic shift in people's lives.)

Forceps people have had the experience that love and aliveness are not safe, and they often get pain and pleasure mixed up. Here is what one forceps client wrote in an email to me: "Before I can really feel any other positive feelings, I need to feel safe, so much so that even IF something is pleasurable but I don't feel safe, I will perceive it as painful and anxiety-producing." And he continues, ". . . [After doing this work] it shows me that I have perceived painful memories that were actually pleasurable. My goal is to go back and relive these pleasurable moments, to convince myself of how good they actually were."

Traumatic births

When pregnant mothers experience trauma at birth (the baby getting stuck in the birth canal, hemorrhaging or mother in extreme pain), the baby is aware of what is happening. "Red lights" are going off all over the mother's body, and she is passing along the fear and panic to the child. The child may pre-verbally decide such things as *If I don't get out of here I will die!, Life is fearful!* or *I am too much!*

It is common for them to be excessively caring for people, especially their mother, if they hurt their mother at their birth. People with this birth-type may have the pattern of turning regular circumstances into dramas, if their birth was a drama and their birth programmed them with that intensity. They may have excessive need to control, feeling the need to overcompensate for the lack of control they had at birth.

If there was trauma that threatened the life of the child, either *in utero* or at the time of birth, when they become adults these people often subconsciously sabotage important things in their lives, such as finances, relationships and health. It is possible they subconsciously have either an intense aliveness intermingled with death, or a life being numb.

What was going on in the world when you were born?

I have an excellent example of a connection between the world outside when you were born and what your patterns are now. I had a man come to me with the extreme feeling that he did not matter. It was a primal, core feeling to him, one which had shown up in various situations throughout his life. In his childhood he was the boy no one chose for games. He was later overlooked in his job for better positions and for raises. Even shopkeepers would overlook him in line, even though he might have been standing within five feet of them.

When interviewing him I learned that he had been born at the exact hour of John F. Kennedy's funeral. You may remember what a dark time that was in our country: Americans everywhere were sad, even sobbing on the street. I assumed that the delivery team for my client had also been sad, or at least preoccupied with our nation's troubles on that day. For a child being born the life force is huge and joyous. When that intense life force is met with an unequal energy, the child makes a pre-verbal decision about the experience.

In my client's case and seeing his life pattern, I assume the delivery team had been thinking about the funeral and might not have had their emotional focus completely on the child. This would have created that feeling of "I don't matter." After working with my theory and my change suggestions (which included doing a Forgiveness Process on his birth team), this man has been able to move that heavy energy and create a more positive view of himself and of life. All healing begins with recognition.

My birth story

My own birth was a few weeks late and I was a large baby. When my mother arrived at the hospital her doctor was not yet there. I was ready, but he was not. The nurses crossed my mother's legs to keep me in as I was crowning, holding back 40-70 pounds of pressure. I had a problem with Claustrophobia for years due to this distressing birth experience. It caused me anxiety to be in an elevator, or in any closed space for long. Even relationships created that feeling in me, of being closed-in. I made the pre-verbal decision "I can't trust support," which has taken me years to work through.

Our birth and womb experiences create templates of how we experience love and commitment as adults. I have written some brief descriptions here of the process I use in my transformational Life Coaching. This unusual process, which incorporates Conscious Breathwork, prenatal & birth information and Forgiveness, can help us find the basic sabotaging thoughts at the core of our negative patterns, and then rewrite them. This is a gentle, powerful & relatively rapid way to help heal life-long negative patterns.

ACTION: Breathe long slow breaths, counting in four counts through your nose and out four counts through your mouth. Do this for twenty rounds. Notice how much more peaceful and relaxed your body feels. Use this process daily to help you remain calm.

You are safe. You are innocent. You are loved.

"Worthy" by Juliana Ericson
www.JulianaNashville.com

Worthy

I am worthy.
God did not create us saying to one person
"You are worthy." and to another "You are not worthy."
We are all worthy.
Every single person on the planet is worthy.
When I remember this, it is easier to see the worthiness in others.
I no longer have to put others down
*   trying to bring them to the level*
*   where I saw myself before.*
I am worthy, now and forever.

– Juliana Ericson

> "He who cannot forgive breaks the bridge over
> which he himself must pass."
>
> — *George Herbert*

CHAPTER 5

Forgiving Fathers

What we learn as children becomes our instruction book for life. During our childhood years we learn details from whoever raised us about relating to our mates as adults. How our mothers treated our fathers, how our fathers treated our mothers, how our parents related to each other and treated us . . . all create templates for us to use in relationships later in life. If we have resentment against our father or mother, we are likely to attract a mate with similar characteristics to what we do not like about that parent. Why?

I believe that Love is the most powerful force in the universe and Love is bringing up those toxic emotions needing to be released and healed, so we can live unencumbered lives. Healing comes through releasing. Anger and resentment rob us from enjoying a life full of love and laughter. We will continue to attract mates and people into our lives who are just like our parents, until we forgive that parent we believe has wronged us. This is a loving universe, and anything not like love will come up in our lives to be released and healed.

A powerful stuffing-it story

This is the story that prompted me to write this book on forgiveness and its transformative nature. I had been hearing forgiveness stories for years from my clients and others, but this one struck me as "scientifically measurable." I felt compelled to record the details and tell others who might not believe that forgiveness was really this magnanimous. I had proof to show that there is a direct and measurable result from doing this Forgiveness work.

Angelina is a confident, successful, cheery business woman. She came to me because she was so in love with her new husband of four years, and wanted to make sure she did not slip back into the previous pattern of sabotaging her loving relationships. She felt she had sabotaged the relationship with her last husband as well as with some boyfriends since her teens. Her previous marriage had been awful and ended bitterly. She had met her current husband, and felt she had "won the lottery," as she put it. Whatever she had done "wrong" before she did not want to repeat. She wanted her sessions with me to be preventive maintenance.

At first it was difficult to get Angelina to open up. She was used to smiling as a mask for her pain. When she'd been a child, her parents had been poor. Her father had worked long, hard hours at a factory job which he hated, but he'd had to work to provide for his wife and three small children. He even expressed it verbally: "I hate my job, and I hate my life! If it weren't for you kids, I'd be doing something else. Maybe I'd even get to have something nice like a Corvette!" He was never physically abusive, but the emotional and verbal abuse left scars on the children, including Angelina.

After hearing some telltale passive-aggressive vocabulary during our initial session, I suggested she do a Forgiveness Process on her father. "Oh no, we're fine," she protested. "I have Sunday dinners with my dad, and we have great conversations. I don't need to bring that old stuff up again."

The next session, I heard some of the same repressed negative words in her conversation with me. Again I suggested the Forgiveness Process on her father. Nope. By the third session, some turmoil had seeped into her precious marriage; I believe her subconscious had created the turmoil, stirring up the repressed feelings so they could be released with the work she was doing with me. (Unresolved feelings with our parents come up in our relationships to be healed.) Her body really wanted to let go of her stuffed anger and it was beginning to seep out again for healing. Her unresolved angry feelings about her father were now coming out as arguments with her husband, who she loved so much! This was new, and it scared her. She finally relented. "Okay! I'll do the

Forgiveness Process on my dad!" she expressed with some trepidation in her voice.

This Forgiveness Process takes about a week. Angelina finished it on a Friday. The following Monday her mother called and exclaimed, "I don't know what's come over your father! He's just ordered a brand new red Corvette!" The guilt she had released had turned into wild abandon. He'd bought his dream car after all this time. The exceptional part about this story is that her father did not even know Angelina was doing the Forgiveness Process, yet he had *felt* the release of long-held guilt from years ago when he'd been the angry father of those young children. (By the way, she and her husband stopped arguing, AND her sixteen-year-old son now began joining them at the dinner table. Don't you just love happy endings?)

Harboring resentments, especially toward our parents, prevents us from experiencing truly deep and meaningful relationships. If your loving relationship is not pleasing to you, especially if you have thoughts of leaving the relationship, give this Forgiveness Process a try. Maybe it is not your relationship at all. Maybe your subconscious just needs some good deep cleaning!

Could a quadriplegic woman do this forgiveness process?

I witnessed one who did, named Marian. She could not move her arms or legs, only her head. She had a beautiful spirit, but since her accident two years prior she had been understandably depressed. I had known her for years and could sense there was an unspoken dark cloud inside that the anti-depressants were not reaching.

I knew about her childhood and wondered if she would be open to a Forgiveness Process. Her mother had become pregnant at 17 as a result a one-night lover, never seeing or speaking with him again. All of her life Marian had felt a desire to meet her biological father. Then in her mid 30s she was excited that her investigating had turned up his phone number. She had wanted to meet him.

During several phone attempts she had assured him she was not interested in his money or disrupting his family or life. Hesitantly he had agreed to meet her for coffee, but for only 15 minutes. She was elated! She would finally be able to look into her father's eyes, see his smile, feel his presence. Marian's life-long dream would be realized! She'd spent a whole hour on her hair and makeup, then put on her favorite dress. She'd driven four hours to the city, to the coffee shop, and arrived a half hour early, just in case. She had waited and waited. No man fitting his description had come into the tiny coffee shop. After waiting two-and-a-half hours, she had called his phone number and only gotten an answering machine. That was the last time she had ever tried to reach him. She had closed and locked that door, or so she thought.

When I suggested now that Marian do the Forgiveness Process on her father, I got the common response: "Oh, I let that go years ago. I don't need to waste time on him." I felt otherwise, and encouraged her to do it anyway. Because of her condition, she could not write so I stayed in the room as she spoke her angry letter, which was the first part of the process. (The complete process is explained in Chapter 11.)

At first she was neutral with her words, then they began morphing into the angry version. After only a few minutes of anger, she morphed into the hurt and abandoned version of her letter. By now, Marian was crying so hard she could hardly speak. I asked if she wanted a break and refused. "No! This poison has been inside me long enough!"

Her toxic venting and crying went on for 45 minutes. I brushed her head for a few minutes and then she peacefully fell asleep. I instructed her on the next part of the healing process, which usually requires writing. Because she could not write, she spoke the words: "One, I Marian . . . Two, I Marian . . . Three, I Marian . . ." and so on. It took her longer and required more mental focus than for others doing this process, but she completed all seven days. I returned on the eighth day and helped her finish the process.

There was a noticeable glow around Marian after that. She emanated a peace, a softness. Her nurse noticed it. Her mother and friends noticed it. What had changed? She had laid her burden down.

I feel we all have one main person, one main challenge, to forgive in our life. In Marian's case I believe she accomplished that. Two months after completing the Forgiveness Process on her father, she died. I believe she died in peace.

Peter becomes his own man

Peter had always worked hard to meet his father's high expectations. His father had never really listened to what

Peter said, and discounted what he did acknowledge. If the subject was not about Peter's unfulfilling corporate job, it was of no interest to his dad. His father only wanted to hear about the bottom line, long-term goals and corporate profits. In his childhood as well as now, his father had spent way too much time at work putting his company before the family. Peter had dreamed of pursuing a music-business career, but instead worked at a corporate job to please his father. He hated every single day working there. Life had become a prison to him, expressing itself as anxiety, depression and a constant skin rash. For years, Peter had felt unimportant and not good enough in his father's eyes. This father-son relationship was strained then and had always been.

After a few sessions with me, Peter was willing to create a positive shift in his life by doing a Forgiveness Process on his father. Peter's angry letter purged pages and pages of emotional toxins from of his body. On a whim, he answered a Craigslist ad, and on the fifth day of the Process he was called in for the interview. The position was for him to work as an apprentice with a producer at a local recording studio. Peter was hired to work weekends. On the sixth day, his father called and asked him to go fishing. Because he had just gotten the exciting apprenticeship Peter said, "I can't. I'm busy" to which his father said "We're both busy. That's why we need to go!" Hearing his father say he would take time from work and ask Peter to go fishing was what he had wanted to hear since he was a boy. On the other hand, this apprenticeship represented the freedom of what he had always wanted to do. It was a difficult decision for Peter to make.

By the seventh day he knew what his answer would be. Peter realized that his father had only been following the tough work ethic taught to him by his father, who had lived through the Great Depression and strained financial times. That was his story. Peter now chose not to follow in those fearful footsteps. He would not put his work before his family, even though the music industry would be joyous to him. He would choose a different path from his father's.

Peter chose to go fishing, and begin the recording-studio work the following weekend. That choice was an ending as well as a beginning. He stepped out of his former low self-esteem by following his own dream and not his father's. He was beginning the new role of being his own man. As he drank in his new empowerment, he was able to see his father as innocent; he had simply been living out the pattern he'd been taught by his own father.

Peter moved beyond the apprenticeship position, learned what he needed to and with great determination and focus began his own business. In the past few years, he has now grown his production company to include music publishing and artist management. He is enjoying every single day of his work life! He and his dad spend regular time now, fishing and watching sports together. Peter's world is brand new. Forgiveness makes all things new.

Juliana,

After our last session, I spent a few days in procrastination, but then completed my forgiveness week on my father. My estranged step-mother is in her 90s and in the last stages of Alzheimer's. Her daughter called me. She said that as she's cleaning out the corners of her mother's house she is finding things that belong to my family. I went back to my family home and collected boxes of letters, pictures, and items that had been saved. It has been a memory trip of huge proportions. I have been able to learn about my father and the challenges he faced with a father and a sister both dying within one year when he was eleven, then his hospitalization in 1944 during the war, to all sorts of other things. I am sad that I was not to know him as I see him in these letters. So fascinating how forgiveness comes about. Not the instant release for me as with the other (Forgiveness Processes) but a gradual understanding of his humanity.

I am now ready to work on my next Forgiveness Process which is myself. The process has already begun." - Candace in Birmingham

Mimi with no regret

While Mimi's father was stationed in Korea, he met her beautiful 15-year-old mother. Her mother became pregnant, although her father returned to the United States anyway. He did send some money to Korea for Mimi's care, but her mother was disgraced in Korean society and had a very difficult time.

It angered Mimi's American grandparents when they

heard about the child and her mother in Korea. Her dad was strongly encouraged to bring them to the United States and marry Mimi's mother. Reluctantly he did so. They all lived with the grandparents for a year until they moved out. That's when all hell broke loose. Mimi's dad began staying out partying several nights a week. He was seeing other women and drinking heavily. If all of that was not enough, he also began beating her mother. Uncertainty and chaos created a sad and fearful childhood for Mimi.

When Mimi was four years old, her mom filed for divorce. Because she was uneducated and unable to provide for her child, Mimi's dad asked for and was given custody. It was not because he loved his daughter. It was revenge against his wife.

By her teen years Mimi's fear had turned into anger and disgust. She remembers him getting drunk, watching TV and passing out every night. "Dad was a mean drunk." She had to cover the bruises and cuts from when he hit her, so no one at school would notice. He made her feel ugly and insignificant by regularly screaming profanities at her. There were times she wished he was dead. He didn't appear to be really living at all. He certainly showed no love toward her or anyone.

Then it happened. "Dad just went crazy one day," and went to the Veterans Hospital. He was diagnosed with post traumatic stress disorder (PTSD), caused from his time there in the Korean War. Mimi stayed with her grandparents while he was in the hospital. Those times were better for her without her father, but she still wanted to leave the family ties as soon as she was able. At eighteen, she had left home and never looked back.

Mimi worked excessively hard to put herself through college. After college, she began earning a good living for herself, making herself proud of her accomplishments. Years later, she learned that her dad had become homeless; he stayed continuously drunk and depressed. She tried to reach out to him several times, but he had no interest and told her to leave him alone.

One time she had sent her dad a bus ticket to travel to her city and stay with her. He then lived in her converted garage for six months. When he began drinking again, she asked him to leave. That was the last time she had seen him in person. She would occasionally see him walking the city streets, homeless. It had been hard for her to see.

Beginning the Forgiveness Process on her father was extremely difficult for her. She still hated him, for what he had done to her mother, for what he'd done to her, for what he'd not done for himself. It took her five months of trying to actually begin the process. She wrote two of the angry letters before she could begin the second part of the process. She finally did it. I shared with her that I was proud of her determination.

Two days after he received her completion letter, her father died of a heart attack in his sleep. I believe there are no accidents. I believe he felt he could only die in peace once he knew that Mimi had forgiven him.

"You've had such a tremendous influence in my life. I don't know where I would be without Breathwork! It hit me the other day, "OMG, I reached contentment!!" I didn't even realize it! I actually like my job. I really feel good about my

*life, I am enjoying being single, I'm really okay
being me where I am at. I feel so good!"*

- Tara, Nashville nurse, after
completing Forgiveness Processes on
both parents, as well as on herself.

Karen and inherited perfectionism

Forgiveness Processes are like peeling layers to get to
our core. Karen needed to find who she was at her core. She
did not know, never had. She had lived a life of pretending
to be perfect for so long, she didn't know who she really
was. She referred to her mother as "Mrs. Cleaver" and her
father as "Mr. Cleaver" (the picture-perfect parents in the
popular '60s TV show "Leave It to Beaver"). Her parents
had looked perfect, acted perfectly, and lived in the perfect
house, but it had all been a facade. The children had been
threatened with beatings and more if they said anything
to anyone. Inside the home there had been intense drama,
hidden from the outside world.

Karen's father had suffered from alcoholism and
intense bouts of anger, drunk or sober. He would throw
and break things, beat her mother, and drug the children
to keep them quiet. He'd been extremely unpredictable
with his temper, creating constant fear and anxiety
for Karen's mother and the children. It had been a very
chaotic and oppressive home life, though all the while
they appeared normal to outsiders.

Karen had two terrible marriages under her belt.
Both men had been physically and emotionally abusive to

her and their children. (We tend to repeat what we have learned from our parents.) When she came to me she was in her mid 40s, depressed and desperate, and had been on anti-seizure medicine for the past thirty years. She had now met a great guy, and wanted to make this relationship work, for once in her life. She was craving to know who she really was underneath the facade she'd become so used to hiding behind. She had done quite a bit of conventional therapy over the years, so it did not take long before she was willing to jump feet-first into the Forgiveness Process. She was tired of pretending, and sure there was an authentic life waiting for her somewhere, somehow!

During her first breath-session with me, her body became as stiff as stone. When the session was over I asked her what she had experienced. "I felt as though I was a marble statue," she replied. "I was observing myself, walking around me as I was this statue. At the end of the session I felt a Divine Spark inside me grow to a glowing fire and burn the marble away. It melted the statue away, and I can actually feel joy for the first time!" She looked radiant. I suggested she do the Forgiveness Process on herself.

During the first part of the process, in her anger letter, she saw herself as a monster. She saw ugliness. In the next part, she forgave herself for allowing herself to be mistreated by her husbands, for buying into the artificial life she continued to live, and for wasting so much time being a victim. She experienced emotions she had never felt before. She was becoming human!

Next I suggested she do the Forgiveness Process on her father. It took four tries before she could even begin the first part. When she did begin, she got violently ill for the entire weekend. During that time, Karen and her new boyfriend got into their first fight, throwing things and being verbally violent with each other, which had not happened in their entire two-year relationship. He asked her to leave; he was not normally like that and it scared her. In fact, the whole weekend was out of control. Karen was vomiting as though she had food poisoning. She was sweating and weak; it was awful! The next day, her daughter came to care for her as she healed. By the fifth day things did get better.

By the end of Karen's Forgiveness Process on her father she felt a new-found peace. She was clear she was not going to allow herself to be mistreated by her boyfriend, as her mother had allowed her father's abuse. She felt what it was like to be empowered, to stop blaming and take responsibility for her own choices and live them. She was no longer living inside her old façade; she was free to choose how she wanted to live. She broke her family pattern of abuse and anger. Karen was free!

(Note: During this Forgiveness Process, many people experience physical reactions, maybe headaches or nausea, or heightened experiences on the fourth or fifth days. By the sixth day, however, things usually get back to feeling better and more comfortable. My best guess is that this is our body purging the emotional toxins.)

Don't forget to finish!

"I realized I needed to do a Forgiveness Process on my dad. He was a super hard worker, provided a great lifestyle for us five kids, but he was never

*really around for me. He never told me he loved
me. I remember just wanting his approval for
working hard, and I don't ever recall him saying
he was proud of me, or thought I did a good job.*

*"Even as an adult I hoped for his approval. I recall
a time when he came out to the family farm. At the
time, I had taken over my in-laws nursery. I had a
gift for growing beautiful hanging baskets, and it
was just before Mother's Day. The greenhouses were
overflowing with gorgeous colors, a few thousand
prime flowering hanging baskets and bedding
plants lined the floors. It was such a sight to see
after months of hard work. I was proud of myself
for working so hard to create such beauty, and I
remember thinking that my dad would be so proud
and in awe. He said nothing. Never acknowledged
the beauty of nature, or how much time and effort I
must have put into creating these baskets.*

*"Over time, I realized that I had married my dad.
My husband is a hard worker, but I always felt
as if I wasn't doing enough to get his approval. I
always seemed to do something "wrong"... just
as it was when I was a child.*

*"I started to do the Forgiveness Process on my dad,
it was going well. I felt great about releasing all
those old resentments, but I did something bad: I
didn't complete the 7 days. Over the next month,
I began noticing my husband's disapproval at an*

all-time high. Not only my husband, though, just about every man I came in contact with. I have several male clients I was working with at the time and there seemed to be a recurring theme. Nothing was going right in my business relationships with men, and especially at home. One day it just hit me: I HAD NEVER FINISHED THE FORGIVENESS PROCESS ON MY DAD!!! There was such disapproval coming at me from so many directions and I realized most of it was the same type of disapproval I had received from my dad. I hesitated no more and completed the FP.

"I learned that my dad was innocent. He had most likely never had approval from his alcoholic father, who would work all day and go straight to the tavern just a few hundred feet from his driveway. I have an appreciation for my father that I didn't have before. I understand that compliments don't come easy or naturally for him, and that's okay. I know he's proud of me even if he doesn't say it."

‑ Susan

ACTION: Notice your "mustard seed." Feel any willingness to let go of your anger toward the person you identified in the last chapter. Don't force it, just notice.

You are safe. You are innocent. You are loved.

64

"Joy!" by Juliana Ericson
www.JulianaNashville.com

Original Innocence

Today I will see myself as innocent
no matter what I thought about myself yesterday.
Today I will recognize that I am a child of God,
created holy in the image of Holiness.
I am still that innocence
beneath the many layers of forgetting
I have unknowingly placed upon it.

– Juliana Ericson

> "To forgive is the highest, most beautiful form
> of love. In return, you will receive untold peace
> and happiness."   - Robert Muller

CHAPTER 6

Children and Forgiveness

In the years before my Breathwork Life Chapter, and before my enlightening process began, I made many choices which were less than supportive to my well-being and to the life I prefer now. One of those choices was to choose the importance of my relationships with men over spending quality time with my young daughter. Shannon saw over and over again how I fell in love, gave my soul and allowed myself to be stomped on by men, leaving me sad and crying. She even had a habit of protecting me when men looked adoringly at me in stores, like she was my little bodyguard. So after seeing this happen her entire life, including with her father, Shannon's last straw was seeing how my boyfriend at the time was emotionally using and abusing me. She could not stand seeing me destroyed one more time!

(I now know that I drew those men to me and created it with my subconscious thoughts, of which I will write more later.)

In desperation, my daughter left. Shannon not only left, she stayed estranged for ten years! She would not answer phone calls, letters, visits, nothing. She refused to see the friends I sent to her office in California on my behalf. She wanted no contact with me, by any means. I was completely cut off from my daughter.

At first I was devastated and thought that I could not go on without her. As the years went by and my attempts continued to fail, the only thing I knew to do was to pray. I prayed daily for years, never doubting they were heard, but not knowing when or how my prayers would be answered.

When I learned about this particular Forgiveness Process, I decided to do one on my daughter. I was angry that Shannon was gone and had forgotten me. So that was the main subject of my "angry" letter in the Forgiveness Process. I decided to send her the completion letter, but as the rule goes, I did not expect a response from her. I was doing this letting-go for me: to be free of anger, guilt, sadness, all of it.

I recorded the date and time in my address book; almost nine months to the day I had sent the letter, Shannon called me. She even had my forgiveness completion letter in her hand while she spoke. She was very, very angry with me. I had two conversations going on in my head simultaneously: one was listening to my daughter spew terrible words at me; the other was praying, asking God to be with me—to give me the right words to say, and to prevent me from defending myself with words that might offend her during a fragile conversation, possibly bringing it to a close. I did not want it to end. It had been ten years!

As I patiently listened, I learned that Shannon was still angry at me for leaving her dad when she was seven and ending that family-time in her life. I was surprised to hear my daughter had harbored such sadness about a time I had almost forgotten. So this gave my Forgiveness Process on her a different twist, one I would have to ponder later. Now I was simply grateful to be speaking with my daughter again.

Over time, we have become great friends again. It's like those ten years never happened. We speak on the phone almost daily and travel to see each other often. Our relationship is open and honest now, sharing our feelings early, instead of stuffing them. She has certainly been one of my greatest teachers.

As an addendum to this loving story, I also did a Forgiveness Process on myself during those years. I had to let to go of the guilt I had about my mothering, or my perceived lack of mothering. It's all good. Love is the most powerful force in the universe. I am certain.

> *"I thought it was going to be tedious and it wasn't! When I get up in the morning it's the first thing I do. I get my coffee and I start writing. I look forward to it. It matters!"*
>
> - Mary Ann, on doing the Forgiveness Process

Forgiving Shannon again

I have had three 50-something female clients lately who became pregnant while attending college and had to quit college to marry. They are still angry about that time in their lives. It has brought up some things I need to let go of that I did not know were still inside of me. My clients were helping me by reflecting my own thoughts, which is how we all can help each other if we are willing to see.

It was January and there was a lot of energy happening in and around me. Out of the blue I got a frantic phone call from my daughter. She said her government checks were going to be discontinued because of a fraudulent discrepancy. (I had not been married when found out I was pregnant; I had had to quit college and marry her father, with whom I was not in love.) People who have been born of an unplanned pregnancy or were born out of wedlock tend to have problems with the government, the law, and other types of authority and legitimacy issues. For years my daughter's hot button was to be wrongly accused of something, or even simply owing for traffic tickets. She would go into a frenzy or experience panic attacks whenever she thought a new job application would investigate her background, even though she'd never done anything illegal. She was subconsciously tied to her life's illegitimate beginning.

So back to the January phone call: Over the years Shannon had sometimes used her given last name. Sometimes she'd used my married name, Ericson. Neither she nor I thought there was a problem with that, since she used the same social security number with each. Well, the you-know-what hit the fan! The government office was now discontinuing her checks because their records showed conflicting names and they felt they didn't have conclusive records that she was who she said she was. They did not have proof that she existed! That was a perfect reflection of my 18-year-old thought of not wanting to be pregnant with her, of not wanting her to exist. She had reached a very deep place in her psyche to be healed. And since she was yelling at me on the phone and blaming me for the whole thing, I was also uncovering a deep place in me still to be healed.

At first it was difficult to hear all of her accusations: that I did not guide her well as a young mother. I didn't do this; I didn't do that. I repeated the same thing I had with Shannon's phone call years ago, praying for peace while I continued to listen to her. After giving my daughter a few minutes to vent, I suggested we continue the conversation on the next day, after she had a chance to cool off. We said goodbye. She cancelled her bi-annual trip to Nashville the following week.

Hearing all of Shannon's words made me realize I still had anger buried deep inside me about when I had gotten pregnant at 18 during my first year in college. At that time I'd had the world on a silver platter: straight-A student, on the homecoming court in high school, popular, studying psychology in college and loving it. Then *boom!* My life hit a brick wall. I had not even wanted to live; I really hadn't. From my 18-year-old perspective, my life was over. I was looking at a prison. I was angry.

I was jealous of other girls my age being able to live life with fun and ease, still being cared for by their parents in that cocoon of carelessness and wonder. Even though Shannon's father was a nice guy and married me after much pleading, my life took on a very different trajectory from that moment on. We stayed together for eight years, then parted. I then discovered that the struggle of single-motherhood at 27 was even worse than being married to a man I had not chosen.

Without going into more detail than you need to know now, I had to forgive my daughter for being born at that time in my life. Of course she was not to blame, but a part of me was still angry, and wanted to blame her for so many unfulfilling years that would have been prevented had I not gotten pregnant. I began the Forgiveness Process the night of her phone call. I wrote the letter, which was *full* of anger and resentment. Then I began the second part of the Process. On the third day, my sister called to tell me that a check I had sent my niece, which I had been given by a friend for something else, had bounced, and that the bank had charged my niece $35. Yes, the check was eighteen months old, and should not have been cashed after that much time had passed, but it was still within my field of experience. Then, on the fourth day (today as I write this), I got a phone call from a woman who still owed me a couple hundred dollars from a Breathwork workshop she had attended last year. She had finally began paying me a tiny $10 the previous month toward her debt. She was calling to tell me not to cash the $10 check I'd gotten the day before, because it wasn't good, and to wait until Friday. THESE WERE THE KIND OF EXPERIENCES I'D HAD AS A SINGLE MOM, WHEN SHANNON WAS YOUNG! I had detested that hand-to-mouth existence.

Those two bounced-check, lack-inspired contacts spoke to me of my difficult past. I now had a prosperous life, but I still carried resentment of having had to provide for a child without a college education, and having to quit that pursuit because I was pregnant. I had had to sell personal belongings just to pay rent. We'd had to eat eggs at dinner for our protein because I could not afford to buy meat. I'd been forced to leave my parents' home where I was being well-cared for, to go live with a man I did not love and who had nothing to offer me.

I wrote in my journal that day:

> *I just finished Day Six today. I feel a lightness, a release from a very deep place. I am looking for miracles today.*
>
> *It is interesting that my friend from college who had helped me when I first found out I was pregnant found me on my Facebook page today. That connection helped me remember some more things I needed to release from that time in my life. Life never ceases to amaze me!*

And from the next journal entry:

> *Day Seven finished. I had a client pay me for sessions two months ahead—first time that has ever happened. It shows me my prosperity-consciousness is loosening up. I was also given a free massage from my massage therapist today. My client this afternoon said that the two*

main points I told him were exactly what his traditional therapist had told him last week; I appreciated being indirectly acknowledged by a college-trained therapist, which I am not. I drank that in.

I have had cramps all day today, which felt like the menstrual cramps I used to have as a younger woman before menopause. Interesting.

In my completion letter to my daughter yesterday I said that because of her I had married her dad who introduced me to a great love of mine: nature. Last night, at a charity event benefiting the environment, the pastor asked that we close our eyes and remember who had first introduced us to our love of nature. Then thank that person. It was Shannon's father. Coincidence? I don't think so!

My daughter called and said she is coming to visit in two weeks. All is well in my world!

ACTION: What is your inner child saying to you today? Listen and act on it.

You are safe. You are innocent. You are loved.

"I Am A Gift" by Juliana Ericson
www.JulianaNashville.com

The Gift

When I begin to have thoughts of anger against my mother
I will remember that she did the best she could
    with what she knew at the time.
She was living with the programming she was taught
    by her mother,
        who was taught my her mother,
            who was taught by her mother.
I know I am free to release my mother and release myself.
I want to build a bridge from my heart to hers.
It's time.

– Juliana Ericson

"At some point you have to move on. You can't blame your parents forever."

- Ilanya Vanzant

CHAPTER 7

Mothers

Resistance to forgiving:

"I've been avoiding the forgiveness work. But I have been thinking about it, and about why I've been avoiding it. I think I need to start with my mother. Not that there's anything huge to forgive. But it feels like if I forgive her, I'll be cutting off an arm, or a leg. I've gotten so used to holding this grudge. When I think about letting it go, I can feel my eyes squinch up, my face grow red, and my feet stomping. Like a 2-year-old's temper tantrum. I don't experience these things physically, but the memory of the response seems to remain in my body. Every time I tell myself I need to just start and it'll get easier, I can feel my cells recoil as if they've been shocked. Maybe now that I've confessed, I'll be able to start. But not tonight..." - Mary, lawyer

Resentment will recur

The resentments you don't clear up with your parents will come up in your other relationships later on. No matter how bad your relationship with your mother is now, or how bad it was when you were a child, the fact is still the same: there was a time when you were inseparable from her. There was a time when you thought your mother was the whole world. You even thought you were part of her! You were enclosed inside her body, feeling her heartbeat, hearing the blood rush through her body, feeling her emotions via chemicals in her/our bloodstream, whether endorphins or cortisol. She WAS your world. Although this kind of bond can be changed and rearranged, it can never be destroyed.

If you want a fulfilling, loving relationship it is imperative that you clear your relationships with your mother and father. The resentment, anger, bitterness you may hold against them will continue to surface in your life through other people until it is purified in your own heart. You will continue to create people with similar negative characteristics as your parent until you forgive them. If for no other reason than to have a loving partner, forgive your mother and father.

Many men attract overbearing, bossy wives who were exactly like their mothers. When these men are asked why they chose women with characteristics that had angered them since childhood, the common response is, "She just felt like 'the one'." That chemistry often feels like fireworks early in the relationship. But once the real reason for the magnetism appears, it can turn the relationship sour. When the bossiness and overbearing nature appears for the purpose of clearing the husband's rage towards his mother, he often misses the lesson. These men do not see it as a chance to heal the relationships with their mothers. They see it as betrayal and disappointment from their wives. Oddly enough, it is at this point when relationships could become absolutely wonderful life partners. About 50 percent of U.S. marriages pass up this opportunity to soar, and they quit the marriage. Husbands could learn a major life lesson here by clearing that relationship. I have heard the term "Our mate is our guru/teacher" and I believe this is true. (I am using the terms 'husbands' and 'wives' because they are representative of a relationship. Of course, these principles are adaptive for all types of relationships.)

For many people, mothers can feel judgmental and controlling even through adulthood. It's not that they mean to irritate, it's just that they learned how to be a mom from their mothers and have probably never questioned it. Their sense of purpose may be tied into motherhood. Or maybe they're living the life they never could live themselves, through their children. It doesn't really matter, because this Forgiveness Process is *our* willingness to be happy and *our* dropping of the rope. The relationship with our mother changes when we change, when we let go and forgive because we simply want to be happy.

I have never dealt with clients who have been brutally treated by their mothers, so I cannot speak from experience on that; However, I have worked with hundreds of people who have been mistreated, unloved and belittled by their mothers. These are the relationships I will be writing about here. In cases of brutal or inhumane treatment by one's parents, my best suggestion is to get professional support to forgive as much as you are able (with no contact), and to replace them in your life with a loving male or female mentor to fill that void.

Apron strings

$150,000 a year. That was Monica's salary. Then she got bonuses on top of that! Not bad for a 30-something single woman with no debt. The problem with this financial equation was that she did not like her job. She felt unfulfilled. She was depressed and felts like a lion in a cage. What to do?

A couple of sessions into her work with me uncovered the root of her depression. Her mother had never agreed with anything Monica did, or chose, or said. From the time of her childhood, her mother was sure she would never amount to anything and would continue to be a disappointment. That's what Monica had used as fuel for her voracious drive in business: to show her mother how wrong she was. One way or the other, Monica *would be* successful!

Love is the most powerful force in the universe, and it is constantly working to clear us of blocks to living life fully. That's what was going on in Monica's life. Her heart was not in it. Her mind wanted revenge, but her heart wanted purpose in her life. Her heart wanted to help others, specifically teenage girls who were lost in their lives.

After finishing the Forgiveness Process on her mother, Monica came to see that her mother was simply living out the programming she'd learned from her immigrant mother, who had learned it from her mother. Once she was clear that mom merely wanted to help her daughter make her life better, unlike the ones she and her own mother had experienced, life opened up.

Monica spent a few months saving for her break. Then she quit her high-paying job, and began working for a non-profit organization helping run-away teenage girls. Life makes sense now and it shows, as Monica actually glows with joy!

Extremely difficult

Helena could not stand her mother; I mean, she hated her! Because of a sense of duty and responsibility to her young son, she had kept in touch with her mother regularly: for 5 minutes, the first Sunday of each month. That was all she could stand. She would put the timer on at the beginning of the call, and when the five-minutes buzzer went off, she said goodbye. Duty done!

Helena's mother had been abusive to her children when they were young. Not only did she scream and yell at them, she also drank to excess, throwing things and raging. Many men were constantly in and out of their apartment while Dad was gone on business, which was often. Helena's childhood had been full of chaos and fear. When one of her mother's boyfriends had tried to rape her as a young girl, Helena's mother had just laughed it off. Add shame and abandonment to her childhood emotional mix.

The only good thing in Helena's life had been her father: she was Daddy's girl. But every time Daddy had

come home, Mom and Dad had fought constantly. All of
that had lasted only a few years, then Dad had left. Helena
then lost the only love in her life, and she had blamed it on
her mother. Before she'd been scared, now she was angry.
That anger had lasted her whole life, until she began
sessions with me.

As usual, I asked her to do a Forgiveness Process on
herself to see the power of this work. She had some issues
with authority she wanted to clear. They were preventing
her from getting along with her boss; she had a lifelong
pattern of arguing with her bosses. She now wanted to
clear her anger with authority, which she improved.

I wanted her to finish one more process before I asked
Helena to do the one on her despised mother: I had her
do it on her ex-husband. Good, juicy stuff there to clear.
Done!

Now for her mother. Helena had completed a few
sessions and had built trust in me, making her more open
than not to the idea. It still took her three attempts to get
past Part One, which is the anger letter. She just could
not bring herself to write it. Her hands even shook as she
wrote those words. After much determination, she did get
through the whole of Part Two. Now, could she focus on
Part Three, the completion letter?

It was not easy. The letter did not just pour out of her.
It was not fluffy and sweet, but she finished it. It was a
couple of minor paragraphs, short and to the point. She
did it!

Often you will find that the largest resistances will
provide our greatest gifts. The gift for Helena was a
mother for her, and a grandmother for her son. The last I

heard from her was that she and her son had just returned from their second trip to be with her mother in Texas, a week each time.

She feels like the childhood stuff has been packed up in a box and sent to another planet. She's now enjoying her mother's wit and personality immensely, and adores seeing her son howl in laughter at the things she does. This is the life she has been waiting for. Helena dropped the rope. The anger and bitterness is no longer worth the pain.

> "After my mom's passing, I chose to do a Forgiveness Process on my mother. This had great intensity for me as she had been abusive on many levels and ways. She had just passed four months before. Two days before she died, a woman showed up in my life whose birthday was just one day off from my mom's. She shared my mom's abusive traits but was also nurturing and helped to support me during the time of making arrangements for the funeral and so forth. On the forth night of the Forgiveness Process the woman who reminded me of my mother locked me out of where I was supposed to be sleeping, and I was out all night on the streets of Manhattan. I walked and walked, processing, understanding, forgiving. I called a friend in San Francisco, and it turned out she'd been locked out also! I was able to support this friend as I walked the streets of Manhattan at 4 in the morning on a cold night. I found out the next day the locking was accidental, but it allowed me to feel what I had felt as a child

> *from my mom. I chose to react differently now*
> *and chose to reprogram my past memories.*

> *"This magical synchronicity became a healing*
> *moment for me. To me, this represented a shift in*
> *perspective, that allowed me to see the positive that*
> *can happen out of challenge: healing, connection,*
> *transformation occurs."* - Mary, Nashville

Mistrust and resentment

Cindy was conceived with one of her mother's lovers without her dad's knowledge. Her mother was gorgeous and a "male magnet," as Cindy described her. The same lover had fathered two more children while her mother's husband was away on his regular business trips. Cindy was the youngest of eight children and there were five different fathers. Her mother had threatened the children with harsh treatment if they told anyone about her lovers.

Cindy was blessed with her mother's beauty, although she was never good enough in her mother's eyes. Her mom's dreams of becoming an actress had never happened, making her forever bitter and resentful. She saw herself in Cindy, who was not interested in acting, yet she projected her unrealized dreams of becoming an actress onto her daughter. Cindy had pushed herself to her limits to be perfect in everything she did, including cleaning the house and cooking meals for the family, even as a young child. It had never been enough. Her mother's volatile temper and heavy drinking had caused a constant chaotic presence in her home. She'd often taken out her rage physically on the children, especially Cindy. At the age of twelve Cindy had begun mixing her mother's vodka with juice and bringing the thermos to school. She'd wanted to numb herself to the life she'd learned to hate.

This gives you an idea of what she had been holding inside before I began working with her: a lot! I knew Cindy would resist the idea, so I waited until our third session to suggest a Forgiveness Process on her mother. I wanted her to work with my targeted affirmations first, to show her how she could change her life experiences just by changing her thoughts. I was pleased when she agreed to begin the Forgiveness Process.

Cindy's six-page angry letter was really toxic! She burned it, and began Part Two of the Process that same day. The first three nights she experienced nightmares and night sweats. She was melancholy and emotional during those days. I explained to her this was like poison exuding from her, and I encouraged her to continue. She did. The nightmares stopped. By the sixth day she had received three high compliments out of the blue from people she barely knew in her office. Cindy was being acknowledged; something was being unraveled in her subconscious. Little things were becoming easier—even great parking places were opening to her. Life itself was becoming easier! The next time she spoke with her mother, *not once* did she say anything negative or derogatory to Cindy. That was the first time in her lifetime her mother had been remotely civil to her.

By the seventh day it was clear to Cindy that the chaotic childhood she had experienced had been the rocket fuel for her being such a fabulous mom to her own kids. It had also fueled her to create an extremely successful business. Her mother's trait of overspending, maxing out credit cards and mismanaging money had shown her how *not* to be. She had learned budgeting and financial planning, using it to better her career and personal life. Cindy's mother's disrespect of her and compulsive dishonesty had made a very honest, trustworthy and respectful woman out of Cindy. She was now at the point where she was almost grateful for the hard road, because she realized how precious her children were.

A man she had known thirty years ago in high school, back when they were both "dirt poor," began calling her occasionally. They would speak for fifteen minutes or so about their day, nothing too personal. On day seven of her Forgiveness Process, Cindy and her old friend had a full three-hour conversation about a variety of subjects meaningful to them both. He was patient, considerate and encouraging to her. Her friend had no children, but had always wanted to be a father. They realized there was a lot in common between them. He invited Cindy and her children to join him at a wonderful resort in Mexico, all expenses paid. As it turned out he was now a mega-successful lawyer, owning three huge law firms out west. He was looking for a meaningful relationship and so was Cindy. Things looked promising!

"The resentments you don't clear up with your parents will come up in your other relationships." Cindy might not have received the relationship her friend was offering, had she not let go of the anger she was harboring against her mother. We must let go of the old to make room for the new.

In another case, after finishing the Forgiveness Process on the mother she had felt was mean and hateful, Amanda sent me this email:

> *"I went to see my mom today (in the nursing home), and the first thing I noticed different was that I was looking forward to it. It did not seem as much like a chore. She was out in the hall as though she was waiting for me. She is ALWAYS in her room, and NEVER been out in the hall. We had lunch together and had a very pleasant visit. Not one button pushed. I did not feel the need to control her and I had compassion for her in her situation. In other words I turned a corner in my relationship with mom. Thank you!"*
>
> - Amanda, Nashville

Only once in all my years

I have only witnessed one of my clients who did not receive a miraculous event or transformation with his Forgiveness Process. That person was a high-powered international lawyer, Harold. I give him a great deal of credit for doing the Forgiveness Process even with his extremely busy schedule. He did three of the processes that did create positive shifts in his life. He credited the Forgiveness Process with his successes about those people. But the one main theme in Harold's life was his extremely overbearing mother. Even though he did two processes on her, he couldn't the feel peace in his relationship with her he wanted. He tried and tried, but could not get on the other side of his anger with her.

Harold's mother had bossed him his whole life, and from what he told me, she had not been a loving or supportive mother while he was growing up. He said she had "sucked the life out of him" and nothing he did was ever enough for her. This was where he was stuck. Harold also suffered from extreme anxiety and panic attacks. There is a possibility he did not want to let go of his anger at her child-rearing inadequacies, because he had used anger as his childhood defense so as not to be completely consumed by her powerful energy. Harold might have felt that if he forgave her and then had no anger as a defense, his lifetime fear of being consumed would actually happen.

I never did find out; he stopped coming to his appointments with me. After I had spent sessions Seven and Eight guiding him toward forgiving his mother, he stopped. I believe he simply was not ready to loosen his anger and let it go. I choose to think that the work he did do on his mother will someday show him some positive results, no matter how long that will take. (I have seen some processes not "flower" for months, even up to a year.)

Another Mom story:

"My stepmother got my letter of gratitude in the mail and my dad emailed back to me on her behalf. He said it could not have come at a better time as she is having some physical challenges at the

*moment. I feel so good about that letter. Life is
really fabulous, isn't it!? Thank you for inviting
me into your magical life, Juliana."*

~ Marilyn, court reporter

Reframing the past with forgiveness

As a child, Marla's nerves were always on edge because
of her parent's continuous quarreling. They would bicker
often, but it was the arguing that had bothered her the
most. She had assumed the role of peacemaker and had
often tried to get them to stop. The fights were usually
about money: Mom saved it and Dad spent it. For years,
they had worked hard to supplement their family income
by flipping houses, buying homes, fixing them up, and
then selling them. However, Marla remembers thinking
as a child that her house was like living in a jail, because
of how her parents' "toxic" relationship made her feel.

As an eleven-year-old, she had gotten in trouble with
the police for stealing $1,000 from a family friend. (Was
she fulfilling her thought of living in jail, or stealing money
to give to her parents so they would stop fighting?) She
recalled making the decision as a nine-year-old to never
have a relationship because of how terrible her parents'
relationship appeared to her.

Fast-forward to the present: Marla is 27 and has never
been in a relationship. She's gorgeous, smart, personable
and has still never had a boyfriend. She's had short term
flings, but just for fun. No commitments.

When Marla began the Forgiveness Process on her

parents, it was to free herself from resentment of all their fighting and for creating the toxic childhood environment in which she had been raised. She wanted to move on with her life.

A friend enticed her to attend a real estate investing seminar; it was Day Five of the Forgiveness Process she was doing on her parents. It was a powerful emotional combination for her to be forgiving her parents, while at the same time learning about the industry they shared for years that had created such animosity in her childhood home. From both experiences, Marla learned a new respect for her parents and their knowledge, as well as the reasons they had bickered.

At the end of the process she also had a new perspective on their relationship. As it turned out, she learned that their sex life had always been great, which might have accounted for the passionate relationship. She also decided that her mom was "nuts, but a good nuts!" Marla now fondly sees her as a Bohemian and an *apassionata*. She imagines her dad as a child, with his own difficult upbringing as well as his time as a captain in Viet Nam during his 20s. She had never stopped to even ask questions about their lives before; it was all about her, always in relation to how they were with her. A whole new light on this arose: a new relationship with her parents to pursue!

ACTION: Try to imagine your mother as a small innocent child. Practice patience and trust the process of life.

You are safe. You are innocent. You are loved.

"Wonderful Surprise!" by Juliana Ericson
www.JulianaNashville.com

Statement of Truth

I matter.
What I am matters.
What I think matters.
What I do matters.
. . . .
I
matter.

– Juliana Ericson

"There is no revenge so complete as forgiveness."
- Josh Billings

CHAPTER 8

Culture, Family Patterns & Formative Archetypes

I have become very interested in coaching people from different cultures and noticing how they vary. The reason for this is that both of my parents were from countries other than where I live, in the United States. My mother was born in Malmo, Sweden; my father was from Kristiansand, Norway. They came to America in their youth, during a time when their countries were not the prosperous places they are today. My parents came looking for work and a "good life," as they put it.

I have noticed varying patterns from different cultures. One of the first international cultures I was able to gauge with a Forgiveness Process was the Middle Eastern one. It is common for parents in the Middle East to prefer having boy babies over girl babies. This prejudice sometimes causes girls to feel inadequate as they grow into adulthood. They can trace their low self-worth as far back as to their prenatal experience. This was the case with Nina.

Nina came from a loving Palestinian family with three children, two boys and a girl. When her mother had been pregnant with Nina, her father had preferred having a boy, although her mother had wanted a girl since they already had two sons. As a child, Nina had been a tomboy and now got along with men almost as equals. She loved sports, dressed plainly and was a hard worker. At the same time, though, she was gentle, lovely and soft-spoken. She had a balance of male and female qualities, so to speak.

The principal reason Nina's father had wanted another boy was to help work in his general merchandise store. She had had to work extra, extra, extra hard to receive any acknowledgment for her competence and intelligence, which were both exceptional. Yes, her father loved her. But in that culture, hard work was ingrained and expected, and men were "better" at doing "hard" work. Nina had contracted Hodgkins Lymphoma at the age of eighteen. She had almost died, but had recovered with chemo and physical therapy. Louise Hay's book, *You Can Heal Your Life*, which I use extensively in my practice, explains that Hodgkins Lymphoma can originate from an excessive need to prove you're good enough. Coincidence? I don't think so. Our thoughts create!

Now we were at the Forgiveness Process part. I suggested she forgive her culture. It was her culture which had spread the belief in superiority of men. I suggested she see that culture as an archetype of a judging, older man. She could not wait to read her angry letter to me, and sobbed through the whole thing. After the reading, she was silent, continuing to cry as it burned in the burning bowl I use for this first part of the Forgiveness Process. Nina told me later that she was feeling the release of all the current and past centuries of women in her culture, right at that moment. She was lost in timelessness. Her eyes were gazing through centuries, and her body was releasing. I could see it in her. It was powerful stuff!

I saw her again a couple of months later. She had a strength of presence I had not seen in her before. Her meekness had blossomed to self-assuredness. Her soft-spoken ways had transformed to openness and directness. Her lack of direction had brought her to a new career, and a move to another city. She had certainly shed her skin, as the snake does when it grows. She was now free to live the life she had wanted, as an enlightened Palestinian woman.

I have seen the Forgiveness Process work on other cultures as well. A Romanian woman who had been born literally "dirt poor" forgave her pre-economic-recovery homeland. Reena had been born and raised in a house with a dirt floor and no plumbing in Romania. She'd always felt unworthy of success and that an easy life was beyond her expectation. The core negative thought she had lived and breathed, that life is a struggle, had literally been bred into her by her extremely poor family and culture.

After her Forgiveness Process, she gradually learned to let in the new life's experiences that had opened up with her forgiveness. She saw how people had begun to treat her with honor and respect. As she let in this new reality, it grew and blossomed in her personal life and her business life. Now she is a changed woman with a prosperous business as she had never before imagined or felt worthy of. She has broken the chains of unworthiness passed on through generations in her tiny, poor village, and sunk into the truth that she is worthy!

Using your breath to encourage the Forgiveness Process

I have had clients from cultures that have taught for centuries for people to stuff their feelings, that it is inappropriate or weak to express emotion. These people have often had a hard time in their first breathing sessions. The breath opens their bodies emotionally and physically, and they have not been accustomed to being exposed in that way.

When people hold in their emotions during a breathing session, it is common for them to experience an unpleasant physical symptom called *tetany*. Their bodies hold so tightly to their thoughts and beliefs, it causes physical pain that can be extreme at times. This tetany ranges from simply stiffness in the jaw or fingers to a whole body tensing, which can be quite painful. Once they let go of the thought they're holding on to, however, the pain usually instantly disappears. It is a great mirror to show how much effort their body has been making to hold on to that unsupportive or negative thought. People who experience this are amazed at how much energy they have spent, holding on to thoughts they don't even want. They've become used to holding so tightly to those thoughts that the tension in their bodies has become normal to them.

When I assist these clients in getting past their breathing blocks, I encourage them to do the Forgiveness Processes. It helps to open bridges to peaceful relationships which had been closed off for years.

Forgiving family patterns

Experiencing a Forgiveness Process on family patterns is similar to doing the process on cultures. The roots are deep and the patterns are multi-generational. As with most subconscious patterns, it can be difficult to find the basic cause, but this process usually gets us in the direction we need to go to receive healing benefits.

You might feel that you are dishonoring your beloved great grandparents, uncles or aunts when writing this angry letter to your lineage. I recommend that you suspend that belief for just one week while you are doing the process. You will experience how much deeper your love can become, when your hidden subconscious resentments have been replaced by compassion and understanding.

I have a couple of examples I want to share with you. The first one is about a nurse who could never get out of debt. Her name was Bridget. She worked hard, and was excellent at what she did, always in demand by doctors and managers. She simply could not keep money in her bank account without spending it. It got to the point where her credit-card debt was in excess of $20,000. She became anxious, had trouble sleeping, became irritable and was even losing her hair. As a nurse, she understood that all of these signs were caused from the stress of her debt being out of control.

My client's anxiety had become unmanageable, but she did not want to take medication for it. She knew it was caused by something in her mind; she just didn't know what. Along with traditional therapy she began sessions with me. As I probed into Bridget's past, she told me that her two great grandfathers had come to the United States from Czechoslovakia, where they had been born into an extremely poor family. Her grandfathers had begun working from their very first day, saving every penny they could to start a business together. They had wanted security for their families and to build a better life for themselves than what they had experienced in their homeland. In five years they both had worked very hard and saved enough money to start a general store.

Their work ethic paid off, and their store became successful within a few short years. The first brother, who was a financial wizard, became overcome with American possibilities, and forced his brother to sell out his store's shares at a reduced price. The first brother then moved the store and his family to Chicago and became a very wealthy man. Over time, however, the second brother could barely provide for his family and they lived a poor existence.

I felt that Bridget had taken on her father's poor family-mind. "I make a good living," she said, "but I still feel poor." In addition to his anger at what he felt had been done to him, her father had always felt inferior to his brother. My client shared that she'd heard him repeatedly say he could never get out of his financial hole. He felt stuck, as though he was still back in Czechoslovakia. In his mind I believe he was. I believe he was still in the poor mentality of his childhood, even though somehow his brother had broken out of that.

I suggested my client do a Forgiveness Process on her grandfather, who had lost his half of half of the store. I felt he had carried the poor-family mind with him to this country and passed it on along to his family here. Shortly after Bridget finished the Process, she was offered the hospital position she had wanted for a while: to become a travel nurse. She would receive a higher salary and get to travel at the company's expense.

I have noticed that with this family mind pattern, people are not likely to make a higher salary than the breadwinner did when they were children. My client broke this pattern when she took the travel nurse job. She began making $15,000 more (in comparative dollars) than her father ever did. She was free!

> *"(After I finished my Forgiveness Process) a little side thing happened as well....When my father died, he left me some things but neglected to mention in his will all the things that were my grandmother's and my mother's. Therefore, my stepmother and her children will inherit our family heirlooms instead of my children. I loved especially a teacart that my stepmother kept by her kitchen table. (Without me asking) her daughter, Barbara,*

called me and said to come pick up the teacart and some silver she'd found with our family initial. So, I guess forgiveness helps in the world of form as well, even though it wasn't my focus in the process."   – Alexa

The second FAMILY PATTERN example I want to share with you is about a woman who inherited a large amount of money from her late husband. Clarissa appeared bright enough, but did not have a clue about how to manage a million dollars. Her parents had come to the United States from Ireland years ago, when Ireland was a poor nation. They'd brought their hard work ethic with them, along with their poverty consciousness. (By 'poverty consciousness' I mean that state of mind when you feel there's not enough money and are strongly connected with a relationship to lack.)

Clarissa's parents had passed on their hard work ethic, along with their belief in lack, to all five of their children. The family was very proud of being Irish, which reinforced everything Irish, including the negative thoughts that were part of their subconscious programming. Over the years, because of various circumstances, Clarissa's parents had lost their house and been forced to live in a tiny apartment. The daughters had scraped by, always living month to month, just as their parents had done.

Then Clarissa fell in love with a wonderful man who adored her. His business grew and became even more profitable after they married. He was a generous man who shared his prosperity with Clarissa's struggling parents. The only thing the couple had ever argued about was money. She had spent it, with no concept of how much spending was too much. Having an abundant amount of money was foreign to her, as though she were dealing with Monopoly money. She'd been programmed with her Irish parents' poverty consciousness, including the feeling of unworthiness when having money.

Unexpectedly, Clarissa's husband died. There was no will, no financial arrangements of any kind, nothing to assist Clarissa with managing this large an amount of money. After the grieving time faded, she became alive again. She awakened to the understanding that she now had a great deal of money, belonging to her and her alone. What does a person with a million dollars do, who has been programmed with a poverty family-mind? She gets rid of the money!

It was too unfamiliar for Clarissa to have that much money belong to her. It did not fit with her subconscious patterning. She gave it away. She spent it. She mismanaged it. She did everything possible to become poor again, which she almost did.

Fortunately, Clarissa stopped herself at the last minute, just before it was too late. First, a friend recommended an astute financial planner who helped Clarissa stop the money hemorrhaging from her bank account. After her initial shock of living with a budget in place, her friend suggested another healing process: mine. She had seen before what Clarissa was doing, and considered there might be a subconscious thought needing to be healed. She wanted to help, fearful that Clarissa would begin spending again, and waste all the money there was left.

We uncovered the Irish poverty pattern from her

parents that had infiltrated Clarissa's entire family. She began to see how she was simply repeating what had been taught to her, as it had been taught to her parents and their parents. Once she saw the pattern, she was more than willing to do the work to reprogram her mind.

Clarissa completed the Forgiveness Process on her Family Pattern, and has since moved to a new level of financial understanding. Her life now reflects prosperity, beauty and restraint. She has found that she can appreciate something beautiful without having to buy it. She enjoys the anticipation of saving for vacations, instead of charging them on credit cards and running up the balances. She now teaches the joy and peace of mind that saving money brings to her. She is passing on a new Family Pattern of financial empowerment.

ACTION: Willingness to break the mold: Breathe in this affirmation 10 times a day for one month: "I can love and respect my ancestors and still be my own unique person."

You are safe. You are innocent. You are loved.

by Nila Frederiksen

Choice Is My Power

The more I forgive, the easier it becomes.
I enjoy the feeling of being in charge of my life,
*   not feeling a victim as I did before.*
I now find it easier to forgive
*   than to hold onto anger and resentments.*
Those negative emotions feel like anvils I must carry,
*   making life unreasonably difficult for me.*
I no longer choose to carry the weight of anger and bitterness.
I know what to do.
I must forgive,
*   whether in the moment or soon after.*
I will forgive, because I choose to be happy.

– Juliana Ericson

"… [F]orgiveness doesn't mean you condone violence; it's that you don't remain angry so that your distress clouds your judgment and leads you to become consumed with bitterness or thoughts of revenge. Forgiveness is an acknowledgment that we live in a dangerous world and have to be safe and need to protect ourselves. It also makes clear that we have to protect ourselves but can choose whether or not to become hate-filled. Ground Zero shows us that even we, as Americans, can suffer damage and attack; which is something that happens all over the world. Indeed, Ground Zero is a reminder of the horror that results when anger goes unchecked. Reflecting on forgiveness at Ground Zero acknowledges we understand what hostility leads to and an affirmation that we don't want to do that."

- Dr. Fred Luskin, Director,
Stanford Forgiveness Projects

> "With forgiveness your victim identity dissolves,
> and your true power emerges—the powr of
> presence. Instead of blaming the darkness you
> bring in the light."   - Eckhart Tolle

CHAPTER 9

Authority Figures & Mean People

Mary and her invisible track-record

Mary was head of a sizable department in a large institution. She had always worked hard, made vast improvements and raised millions of dollars for the institution's nonprofit division. My client had been with her company for almost 25 years, and it hurt Mary tremendously that her company had never properly acknowledged her accomplishments. In addition, her boss was condescending to her, did not include Mary in important board meetings, and was sometimes downright rude to her. All-in-all, she found reasons to judge her boss for his shortcomings and to feel resentful. This had gone on for most of her twenty-five years with the company.

Mary had been a forceps birth, so I

suggested she do a Forgiveness Process on her obstetrician first. Our obstetrician, or whoever delivers us at our birth, is our first authority-figure. How we were treated during the delivery by that person creates part of the patterns of how we deal with authority later in our lives. I wanted Mary to see how this Forgiveness Process can improve relationships with people we may not even know, but who have directly influenced our lives. I chose this subject because she had been having such trouble at work with her boss. In fact, the pattern with her boss was one she'd had with other bosses: feeling victimized and manipulated by them, having her bosses overlook her and not acknowledging the hard work she had done for them, and Mary was angry about it.

Anger with authority is a common trait of forceps-birthed people. This originates from being painfully manipulated at birth by the doctor. (Nine months of bliss in the womb, then an extremely painful birth using forceps.) Often the person has a pre-verbal thought that the doctor has disregarded the child's pain, and may subconsciously hold anger against any and all authority for years, or even a whole lifetime.

Within a week after she'd finished the Forgiveness Process on her obstetrician, Mary called me, so excited and giddy! She had received a national award for a low-budget advertising program she had designed. The head of the national organization had contacted her boss, raving about my client. Mary's boss had then asked for a meeting and told her in person how much he appreciated her and all she had done for the company over the years. She was struck with amazement and felt as though she were dreaming. After that, she began noticing upper management treating her with more respect and equality. My client even received a few notes of acknowledgment from them. Mary had moved to a new level.

She told me that a major grant that she had wanted for years was given to her company, acknowledging all credit to Mary and the work she had done! She made a point to forward the email to her two superiors. She learned that while she had removed the block of anger of being manipulated and disregarded by her obstetrician, she now had to take charge of her life direction as the adult she had become. She began directing information to her bosses, so she could be sure they knew about her follow-up successes.

My client no longer had to blame her boss and the "higher ups" for how angry she had used to feel toward authority figures. Along with anger at her boss and her company, there was anger at herself for feeling helpless and inadequate, and not moving ahead. She had allowed blaming others to prevent her from moving forward on her own.

After Mary forgave authority, and then herself, she realized that she really was in charge of her own life and acknowledgments. She dropped the rope and stopped blaming others. She was in charge of her own life, and she was free! Mary doesn't feel like a victim anymore, as she had her whole life. She now knows she can take charge of her life and can be her own authority!

"Once I did the Forgiveness Process on my obstetrician I've noticed I haven't had an issue

*with getting up in the morning for work and I
haven't been late once. I mean it hasn't even been
hard to do, I just feel like that issue is fixed."*
- Christen

Mean white men

Latisha was brilliant. She had two Masters' degrees
from fine Ivy League universities, and was working on
her doctorate. She had accomplished all of this as a single
mom while working two jobs.

Being a black woman in the South in the 1970s had
its challenges. Being a brilliant, Type A black woman
in the South was a whole other experience. Latisha had
been treated with a condescending tone at every turn
when looking for work. She had been denied employment
several times for various, shallow reasons. Her time at
both colleges had been made unreasonably difficult by
the men who were supposed to be helping her. Latisha
had been given college plans by her advisors that would
be almost impossible even for near-geniuses. All of these
obstacles and mistreatments had one thing in common:
They all came from Caucasian males, or "mean white men"
as Latisha called them.

Latisha's parents had struggled their entire lives just
to get by. Both had had superiors in their jobs who were
cruel or mean, and Latisha's parents had blamed those
bosses for the lack of their prosperity. Her parents had
passed on their beliefs about condescending white men
to Latisha.

And that was how Latisha had stayed stuck, no matter how hard she had tried, no matter how high her grade point average had gone, no matter how many awards she'd received. She was stuck in blame and victim-thinking. I suggested she consider white men as an archetype, and forgive them as a group.

At first, Latisha simply resisted the idea. Then she got sick and could not begin the process. Then she had company coming into town and could not start. After that, she had a huge report to write and said she did not have time to do the Forgiveness Process. Our egos can be very persuasive. They can be very creative in how to try to prevent us from letting go of what has been holding us back! When people get to this point I suggest they ask for help, to do what they have to if they want to move through this stubborn resistance. (*Remember the mustard seed? That's all the willingness you need to move forward.*)

She did ask for help; Latisha called me. A major way I help my clients is to support them in moving through their resistance to forgive. She requested two sessions with me that first week to support her breakthrough process. My client finally finished the whole thing! And what was her gift? The first one was that her "mean" college doctoral mentor was "mysteriously" replaced by another white male, a world-renowned scientist in his field, which was a real plus for Latisha in career terms. His easy and supportive manner helped her relax into the doctoral challenge ahead of her, helping Latisha to finish earlier than expected.

During this time, her personal life also got easier. A wonderful man came into her life. For the first time she was experiencing a gentle, intelligent, helpful and supportive man (who happens to be white). She could relax now, and not have to prove her worth to anyone. Forgiveness often comes bearing surprising gifts!

After arguments and lawsuits over trying to adopt her four year-old step-daughter for two years, another client decided to complete a Forgiveness Process on the birth-mother who had not wanted her. This is the email I received the following week:

> *"I just wanted to let you know that I completed the Forgiveness Process on my daughter's birth mom. Then, the day after that I received notification from my attorney that we have a court date of April 11th to finalize Nya's adoption. :-)"* ~ Tina

A forceps-birth client explains his breakthrough & gifts:

> *"It is an amazing thing that Juliana did for me. She made it incredibly safe for me to go all the way back to my birth, and see why I've lived the life I lived up until those sessions with her. She helped me bring to consciousness these very destructive things I've put myself through and blamed everyone else for. It has been very empowering to accept that I did this to myself. Many therapies take you through a process, where you remember what happened and see you were a victim of circumstances (difficult parents, etc.), and you*

ultimately forgive them, if you want to live your life. But there was a piece missing here, and it is what kept me crashing and burning. That piece is that I did this to myself, and if I forgive myself for this, then I reclaim my power. This is straight out of 'A Course in Miracles,' which I was deeply into before I met Juliana.

"In Breathwork I really got that I did this to myself. This gave me the ability to forgive myself for what I did to myself, and forgive myself for attacking my parents, by forcing them to drive me to get me to do what I wanted. Pretty nuts huh? This is such a common thing among forceps babies. We get others to force us to do what we want to do. Then we get angry at these people, and we push back and screw ourselves over. It is so insane, because it feels emotionally as if we are always being forced to do what we don't want to do, when we are actually making others make us do what we want to do. It is bringing this to consciousness by breathing into all of these past feelings and events and re-experiencing them that frees us from this cycle of blaming others for what we've done to ourselves. This is especially painful as an adult, because this screwing ourselves over has nothing to do with what we're going through in the moment, as we are making those around us wrong. We turn on someone who gives us exactly what we want, and they don't have a clue. They leave feeling attacked and not knowing why, and we

make it their fault. But because it was our fault, we are left with massive guilt, which we have to put a huge heavy lid on.

"Juliana took the lid off of my guilt, and then showed me I had to forgive myself and everyone else I was holding a grudge against. Even though I had done all of this to myself, I had to forgive everyone in my life who had caused me pain, from the obstetrician to my parents to my brothers. Of course, these people had only given me what I asked for, but since I had not believed this for years and years, I had to go through the Forgiveness Processes with Juliana. I really looked at why I was still so angry at these people, and forgave them for being as hard on me, even though I had cajoled them to be hard on me.

"Ultimately after all of this forgiving others, there were two beings I had to also forgive to complete this whole Forgiveness Process, God and myself. In 'A Course in Miracles' we are confronted with the truth that we turned against God, and in an act of pure and total projection, we blamed our whole self-created mess on God. We then really set ourselves up for our perpetual fear of God, always afraid He/She is going to strike us down at any moment for being such bad Sons/Daughters. But God is love, and since we are doing this to ourselves, we can only return to God, if we forgive God and ourselves for what we never did. This

means we forgive ourselves for the grudges we have held against God and ourselves, so we can complete forgiving all of our enemies and get on with living an easy life.

"The result of a forceps baby bringing all of the reasons for his anger to consciousness is to forgive everyone and stop resisting what he wants to do. In letting go of resisting what I wanted to do, I did it and allowed it to be done for me. Around my ninth session with Juliana, she was really making me aware of how much I resisted life and how easy my life could be. Simultaneously, I was running out of money and was in despair that I would have to stop seeing her, just as I was beginning to see the light at the end of the tunnel. In a fit of open hopelessness, I raged at God that I needed help so I could complete my work with Juliana. It Came! I was sent enough money to do what I wanted for an entire year. This was a miracle. You have to understand how huge this was for me. I had grown up practicing endless hours on the guitar. I believed I only got what I worked endless hours for. I wanted miracles of ease in my life, which 'A Course in Miracles' promised me, but until then miracles were never for me.

"At this point I began seeing Juliana two and three times a week. I told my family about this miracle, and some of them were in shock, couldn't comprehend what had happened. Within a few

weeks, I made a decision to leave Nashville and move to Albuquerque. When I told Juliana of my decision to leave, she asked me how all of my other moves in my life had been. I told her they had been incredibly difficult and exhausting. She told me moving was the same as our birth. I had been forcepsing myself out of every place I moved from, it was always extremely difficult. This time had to be different, and it was! I let professional movers move me, and the movers delivered my things to Albuquerque a day early. My life was reflecting ease for the first time in my life." ~ Tim

In charge and hating it

"I have to be in charge of everything in our family. I'm sick and tired of it!" This was the first thing out of Melanie's mouth when she sat down for her session. She was in charge of most of the details in her family: her son's extracurricular schedule, picking out the new family car, where the family would be going on vacation this year, where their new garage should be built . . . she even took care of the accounting books for her husband's business. Even though he resented her controlling ways, her son expected his mother to choose the college he would be attending, help him sort out arguments with his friends and provide food for his buddies when they visited for their regular weekend TV sports viewing. The family's relationship had been strained for years because of Melanie's bossiness, but her husband had chosen not to make any households decisions, not even choosing which movie to see or in which restaurant they would dine for the evening. She had made them depend on her and that is how the family ran.

Melanie was in charge of it all, but not enjoying the process as much as she once had. She was sad and lonely. She was ready for things to change, but had not a clue about how to do that. If she did change, how would her family fend for themselves? How would her husband's business survive? Would her son go out to unsavory places to get his social fix if she did not provide the weekly sports parties? She felt responsible for them, and felt she had no other options than to keep going on as she had for years. A problem with this picture is that Melanie was not taking time for herself, and the lack of fun in her life was taking its toll. She was tired a lot, she had no sparkle and her body ached. As she was running everything for her family, Melanie was running herself down.

I sensed an energy about her that I will describe as "needy," in addition to her suppressed underlying anger. Melanie often smiled as an automatic response to cover up her negative psychic barbs, but people could definitely feel it. I believe that was a major reason why she complained of having few friends. Most communication is nonverbal, so this offensive emotion is easily perceived by others, even when the sender is pretending not be angry.

As I have mentioned earlier, this anger energy is fairly standard with people who were delivered by forceps. Another common trait of people experiencing this beginning is that they feel more comfortable being in charge and do not like being controlled. Deep down they feel that no matter how much they do, it is not enough. This thought originated from their helplessness at birth, hence having to be pulled out. They subconsciously overcompensate for their primal fear of not being enough by being in control as much as they possibly can. These forceps people try to overcome their fear of being hurt again, as the forceps hurt them, by doing it all themselves. This is where Melanie was. Even though it was draining her, she felt an overwhelming urge to control everything. In her deep subconscious, she felt she did not want to again experience the primal fear she had felt at birth.

My client became nauseated on the fifth day of the Forgiveness Process on her Ob/Gyn, and had to return home from doing her husband's accounting work at his office. She had to lie down. While she rested, Melanie sobbed as she remembered all the times in her life where she had pushed herself so hard to stay in control of things that she became sick. Controlling too hard and pushing people away, it was all beginning to make sense to her. She could feel the energetic shift beginning to move in her body. For the first time she could remember, Melanie was feeling hopeful. She took time to do the required writing on the day's Forgiveness Process, then fell asleep.

On the seventh day she got a phone call from an old friend, asking her to attend an art opening with her the following weekend. This was an amazing occurrence since Melanie had not gone to a social event with a friend for several years. She was also surprised when her husband offered to make dinner that evening, so they could catch a movie he wanted to see. This was all so new to her, she could hardly catch her breath!

Over the next few months Melanie's husband began evolving into the attentive and loving man he had been toward her at the beginning of their relationship. Her son and his friends alternated their Sunday-afternoon sports TV watching between her house and a friend's fully-stocked media room. She began creating time to regularly attend social outings with friends, understanding the importance of how it would improve her outlook on life and her place at home. Her life was opening up. As she let go of control, and continued her positive affirmations and lifestyle, she was creating a healthy new life for herself.

ACTION: Look for your own resistance to authority: a boss, a civic leader or just "the government" in general. Does your resistance strengthen or weaken you? Is the struggle enough to entice you to complete a Forgiveness Process on that authority figure?

You are safe. You are innocent. You are loved.

"Joy Party!" by Juliana Ericson
www.JulianaEricson.com

The Miracle

I am determined to see my story differently today.
I am determined to find any bit of good
there may be hidden inside my story
that I did not see yesterday.
I want to leave the world of blame and victimhood
to join the world of freedom and aliveness.
I want to live!
Here I come!

– Juliana Ericson

"When you hold resentment toward another, you are bound to that person or condition by an emotional link that is stronger than steel. Forgiveness is the only way to dissolve that link and get free." - Catherine Ponder

CHAPTER 10

Addicted To Pain And Suffering

You may have experienced a newfound friend asking, "So what is your story?" You know they mean, "What is the main negative experience you have that is still running your life? What awful thing happened in your past that you continue to re-live repeatedly in your mind?" It could have to do with your parents. It could be about a lost love. It might be about something a stranger did to you. The fact is, we all have a story. It is constantly running in our subconscious, either close to the surface or hidden deep behind locked doors. Some repeat it over and over again, wearing out their loved ones with continuous bitterness and resentment. Others might push it deep down inside and never discuss it.

Our story is another way of saying "I am

a victim." In our story we are the loser; someone else did something to us that we did not like. In our story we were helpless to help ourselves; it's a story of good versus evil, and we were the good character. When we relive our story for many years it lodges victim-thinking firmly into our subconscious. It is reinforcing inadequacy and helplessness in our minds. When we hear something this many times we believe it is true. We believe we are helpless, a loser, and so on. What we believe is how we live, how we create our experiences. Is this how you want to live, really?

All of the accounts in this book are meant to inspire you to move past your own blocks to the peace and happiness beyond. Have you ever imagined what your life would look like if you did not relate to your story? Can you imagine living in the present, not bringing your past hurts into this moment? It's certainly worth your time to notice any resistance you have to these questions. This resistance may appear harmless, but it's like a monster protecting and in charge of your resentful, revengeful feelings. This monster controls you with fear, making your subconscious feel that you would disappear into oblivion if you let go of the anger-hold you have on past wrongdoers.

Do you realize that when you are frustrated, angry or miserable, you create your own hell? It's true that too often, we simply don't want to acknowledge and take responsibility for our experience in life, preferring to shift the blame for our funkiness to someone else. But here's the reality: by comparing your experience in the moment with that of some imaginary "perfect" moment, you disconnect yourself from appreciating all that this present moment holds for you, including humor, humility, empathy, acceptance, learning . . . and even bliss.

Not only is your judgment of the situation making your life hellish, it robs you of the power from which you can do something to change the next moment. Think about this: when you want to make a change in your life, is it better to come from a negative or a positive context? If you want to change a bad habit, do you think that if you beat yourself up long and hard enough, you'll finally make the change you'd like? Instead, would coming from a position of good humor and acceptance get you to your goal faster? Most will agree that it is a more pleasing experience to be nurtured than to be scolded. In other words, loving support is a position of power. Try it.

Suffering was a normal experience

I had a client I had known for years. She and her family are wonderful people who are as service-minded as any people I have ever known. They give and give and help and help. All the while, Joanne has had a dynamic, full time job, a 23-year-old son (who's given them his share of problems) and a special-needs teenage son who could not stay alone, needing help with even small personal tasks. I was having coffee with her one day meeting about a service project we were working on together.

"May I share an observation with you?" I asked. She agreed. "With all you have going on in your life, I wonder if you're as calm as you appear. Joanne, are you holding something inside o you that needs to be released?" I asked her lovingly.

"So what do you think I have inside of me?"

"Anger that life has to be a struggle," I answered. "And I think you don't even realize that anger is inside you." I explained about only 15 percent of our mind being conscious, with the other 85 being subconscious. She was curious, because she had not been sleeping well for a time and had been silently suffering with a great deal of anxiety.

Soon Joanne began her series of sessions with me, and she was amazed at the power of this conscious-breathing technique. What she was even more amazed about was the huge number of constant miracles that came into her life as she completed the Forgiveness Processes. She had been raised on a working farm where a great deal of hard work had been expected from everyone in the family. That was not where she was stuck; cooperation and working together is a good thing. My client's problem came from her mother's constant criticism and negativity.

After Joanne's current authority issue was cleared (involving the overwhelming negative influences appearing in her life at the time), it was time to go deeper into her subconscious patterning. She saw the profound and immediate effects of the Forgiveness Process magically appearing in her life. She was then willing to begin one on her mother, even though she had originally resisted. It was a difficult concept for her; she was, and had always been, a devout Christian, using the Ten Commandments as a guide in her life.

It was hard for her to get past that 5th Commandment

("Honor thy mother and father") and write the anger letter. I explained that this Forgiveness Process would remove the blocks that had prevented an acceptance of and loving closeness to her mother for most of her life. I went on to say that their relationship would most likely improve beyond her imaginings. I reminded her that in the Bible Jesus speaks of forgiveness almost one hundred times, more than any other subject. I told Joanne that the resentments and anger she was hiding toward her mother kept her from unconditionally loving her, so in a way she was not really loving her mother at all. She began the anger letter.

By the fourth day she got sick: vomiting, headache, fever. She had to get medicine from her doctor. When Joanne called to report what was happening, I told her I suspected that anger and resentments were being dislodged and flushed out of her body because of the Forgiveness Process. I encouraged her to take care of herself, but to continue forgiving, along with warm aromatherapy baths, soothing music and her medicine. The physical sickness subsided in three days, and Joanne *tried* to write her completion letter. I say "tried" because she read it to me during her next Coaching/Breathwork session, and it was still full of jabs and suppressed resentment. She wasn't surprised when I told her it was not a "clean" completion letter. I asked her to burn it and do another one. Her next attempt was a little better but still a *no-go*.

By the third attempt, Joanne had become aware of how she carried her "story" with her through the years. She was aware of how she still blamed her mother for her hard life (the struggle pattern she'd learned from her, and which she continued to choose as her own path). Joanne was also aware of how hard she was on her son, just as her mother had been on her. She figured that was one of the reasons he rebelled with his antics. She became aware that her mother was simply judging and setting high standards because that was what she learned from her own mother. Joanne now let go of the judgment she had put on her mother for so long, and began to really see her. For the first time that she could remember, she began to enjoy her mother's company.

> *"True forgiveness is not an action after the fact, it is an attitude with which you enter each moment."*   - David Ridge

What I have seen in my career is that it's not simply enough to intellectualize our way through relationships such as Joanne's. It doesn't help to just say, "Oh well. I know she had a hard life as a farm wife, and was the oldest of six kids in a poor family. I understand why she was that way." That's not enough information to shift our anger or the resentment we hold in our bodies. We need to get our emotional body involved and to feel the feelings again, in order to release them. Those feelings are still there after all the years, after all the books we've read, the workshops we've attended and the successes we've attained. It is as though those thoughts have been frozen in our energy field until we transform them.

I choose to use Love as the transforming tool. *A Course in Miracles* says, "Forgiveness is a choice we must make,"

This is because Forgiveness frees us from our past hurts by bringing us right into the present moment. How can we really be present when we are angry or hurt about something that happened years ago? Or guilt from years ago? Guilt demands punishment. If we feel guilty we lash out, expecting the other person to retaliate, and that can set up a vicious angry cycle that may last for years. It's just not possible to be present in the moment while at the same time being angry at someone about something done years ago. We cannot be in two places at once: then and now. Choose "Now" with forgiveness and let go of the past.

Another common trick of our ego is to instigate thoughts such as "I'm feeling bad, sad, unlovable, etc. I have to find someone to blame for how bad I feel. It isn't my fault for how awful I feel, it's theirs!" Then we hold that person hostage so we can have a reason for why we feel so bad. Our ego LOVES to set up these tricky prisons. I say 'prisons' because these set-ups really are prisons in that they keep us from going out and experiencing life and love fully. These prisons can be in the shape of a hamster wheel, where we relive the same painful event over and over and over again, not ever realizing that we can simply step off the wheel at any moment. They can also be like concrete walls, preventing us from feeling life and love, with us not realizing that the door to the prison is unlocked; we merely need to open it and walk through.

During this time of imprisonment we usually find other prisoners in our darkness. Carolyn Myss refers to this communication as "woundology." We befriend others who speak the same language of wounds, pain, betrayal and loss. "My husband left me for his secretary, too," can be the beginning of a friendship between two women, who will continue to bash their husbands and men in each other's presence. It's the way they bond. I'm not suggesting that friends should not share their pain. What I am saying is that it's unhealthy to stay in that blaming and belittling energy for long. It keeps us in the past. Notice how much of your communication is about past pain. Are you addicted to *woundology*?

A story within a story

Her parents were teenagers, got pregnant and then everything fell apart in their family. Amora's life had been one rejection after another. It began when she was in the womb. Her parents were still in high school and the news of pregnancy was the last news they had wanted to hear, for at least another five years. They were apprehensive about telling his parents, but *afraid* to tell hers. Amora's grandmother, her mother's mother, was the matriarch of the family, and she ruled with an iron hand. She could be generous and loving, but her rules were *the* rules.

Amora's parents had practiced what they would say to her parents, cried and practiced some more. They had decided they would get jobs at night while continuing school during the day. They would somehow make this untimely roadblock in their lives work. The father could help out at his uncle's drugstore, delivering prescriptions. Mom could make money babysitting for people in the community. They were hoping they could live with

Amora's maternal grandparents for a couple of years to save money; Amora's father's parents lived out of state.

The young couple had explained their sticky situation, along with their plans. Amora's grandmother had jumped up and screamed, "Get out of here!" She had wanted nothing to do with her pregnant daughter, nor with the expected granddaughter. She had considered it a sin and an embarrassment to her family. Amora's mother had been devastated. Her mother had then called her mother for help. Amora's great-grandmother had reluctantly agreed to help them for a few months.

When Amora had been born, there had been no preparation for her. There was no crib, no toys, and only a few necessary clothes. Her "crib" was one of the drawers from an old dresser from the attic, covered with a blanket. Amora's grandmother had not come to see her until she was four months old, even then she had not been nurtured, only acknowledged.

That was how Amora had created her core belief of "I am not wanted." This belief had not begun in school, although it had certainly surfaced there repeatedly by rejection from the other kids. This core belief had begun in her mother's womb, at her birth and in the first few months of her life. A most unusual thing had occurred at Amora's birth. Her mother had told her, "You tried twice to climb back in!" It had been as though the baby knew she was not wanted, knew she had created a situation that was eruptive and wanted to go back inside her womb where she was safer.

Amora has been one of the most tenacious clients I've ever had the pleasure of working with. She began feeling an emotional rumbling after her first session with me. Although she did not know what she was feeling, she knew it was different from what she was used to feeling, and it was good. Instead of the usual first one on forgiving herself, she chose to do the first Forgiveness Process on her grandmother. She had a huge amount of bitterness and anger stuffed inside. Her grandmother's rules of "pretend it didn't happen" and "smile, even when you don't mean it" had been mandatory in her family. Amora had spent her entire life giving in to others and not expressing her own needs and desires. She was used to rejection and used to being insignificant.

This pattern of rejection, unworthiness and not feeling wanted had extended into her twenties. Amora had attracted boyfriend after boyfriend who mistreated her and devalued her. By the time she came to me, she actually thought it was okay for her then-current boyfriend to spend the whole evening texting on his cellphone, without answering any of her questions or speaking at all. After that he would have a quick sexual encounter with her, then leave. She was used to being devalued, to not getting the love she needed and inwardly craved.

Over her time with me, Amora finished many Forgiveness Processes. She did one process on her grandmother, on herself a couple of times, one on her mother, her father, some on a few old boyfriends and one on her sister. Each one unraveled another new insight into her previous self-created character weaknesses. Each one created more of her solid self-worth. Amora discovered there were things she wanted to do in her life that she had never considered, because she was always trying so hard to please other people. She began dreaming of her future, something she had never done. Life had been so difficult she had not even felt worthy of dreaming!

It was interesting for me to hear about the progression of her boyfriends' qualities over that year; it was a mind map of what she was releasing and moving toward. The last one I heard about sounded like a really kind and gentle fellow. He made her feel safe enough to open her heart to love. That was a first for her. She was now clear she did not have to give her body as an exchange for minor recognition. This man valued Amora and because she had done enough work on herself to know she was worthy, she received his gift to her.

Her story has been her identity

Maria had been in therapy and counseling groups for years. She had told her story maybe a hundred times before she came to see me. She had always chosen unavailable men for her relationships. It had to do with how she related to her father, as well as her expectation of what a loving relationship really is.

Maria told me about how her father had been attracted to her budding sexuality when she was still a preteen. He was condescending toward female intellect and abilities, but was complimentary of women's sexuality, including hers. She said he had "underestimated her humanity" and contributed greatly to her low self-esteem. In addition, her father had not been available to her emotionally as he had been when she'd been younger, and Maria had been starved for that connection.

My client had a general distrust of men, and often expressed unexplained anger. This had been a pattern since her teenage years. She did want to recognize that it could have had something to do with her thoughts about her father. The story Maria repeatedly expressed for years had been her security, and she was unwilling to see her life differently. I suggested she read the book "Silently Seduced" by Dr. Kenneth Adams. It had been recommended to her in counseling before but she had resisted. Maria knew she was willing to read it now. She knew she had to confront what had been happening and move on with her life.

Shortly after that session Maria became willing to forgive her father. She wanted a healthy loving relationship and understood that her unhealthy feelings about her father were standing in the way. In the first few days of her Forgiveness Process she wrote seventy *different* things to forgive him for. They were very specific. By the sixth day she was down to only two things to forgive.

Maria began to notice a change at work in how she interacted with male co-workers. She now felt more confident around men, more of a competent equal. One interaction was especially pronounced: to a man with whom she had felt major tension whenever they communicated, she now felt nothing. Before she had cringed when she even saw him, now there was simply a neutral feeling.

When her boss asked for volunteers for a difficult project, Maria raised her hand. She felt empowered to see she was the only woman on the team of four men. These were bonuses she experienced: she expected to open up to a loving relationship, not realizing the relationship would be with herself.

ACTION: Investigate what your "story" has been.
　　- Forgive yourself, then take steps to stop your story.

You are safe. You are innocent. You are loved.

"It's Safe to Let Go" by Juliana Ericson
www.JulianaNashville.com

I Am Safe

In my inner core
        I feel safe.
In my body
        I feel safe.
As though cool water is being poured upon my soul,
I release guilt and judgment, feeling safety blossom within me.
I no longer have to defend myself.
Fear is banished from my life.
I no longer have to feel anxious about retaliation.
I am safe
        because I have forgiven.
I can put down my sword.
I am safe.

– Juliana Ericson

"Forgiveness does not change the past, but it does enlarge the future." - Paul Boese

CHAPTER 11
Challenging Relatives

Do you have relatives you wish were related to someone other than you, and you would never have to see again? It's pretty difficult to have holiday gatherings, family weddings, graduations and the like when you have to be around family members you cannot stand to interact with. I will show you another way to deal with your incorrigible relatives that is much easier than other ways you have imagined. Take a breath . . . and forgive them! The more you do not like this idea, the bigger the gift you will have when you do it. Here is an example of what I'm writing about:

Malicious mother-in-law

Pearl is married to a wonderful man, has a great marriage, a great life. What is the problem? Her mother-in-law. She has always felt that no woman was good enough for her son, and *definitely* not Pearl. So every time they visited his parents, Pearl got her feelings hurt. Mom-in-law either spoke to Pearl with a degrading tone or ignored her altogether. (This might be easier to understand with a newly married couple, but Pearl and her husband have been married twenty five blissful years!)

Negativity will chip away at our emotional body over time. That can make us apathetic, anxious, unmotivated, depressed and even hardened. Because our physical body includes and takes its signals from our emotional body, we can get sick from this constant eroding. That was what had happened to Pearl: Her mother-in-law's degrading treatment on her for all of those years had taken its toll. Whenever she and her mother-in-law visited, or even spoke on the phone, Pearl developed hives and psoriasis.

I suggested she should do the Forgiveness Process on her mother-in-law. Pearl actually shrieked in disbelief. Forgive someone who had treated her like a dog for 25 years! I reminded her that a large resistance would bear her a large gift. She was tired of the years of struggle and was intrigued there might be another way out of the painful enmeshment she had battled for so long. She began a Forgiveness Process the following weekend, on her day off, writing a most scathing angry letter.

On Day Four she called me, complaining of nausea and a headache. She wanted permission to stop. I told her she was feeling her own resistance, and that I hoped she would continue. I suggested she first care for her body in whatever way she needed, but that she continue the

THE OTHER F WORD

writing process. It is common for people working on this Forgiveness Process to have physical or emotional responses on Day Four. I liken it to climbing a mountain, and on that day you've reached the top of the mountain with all of your emotional baggage. On Day Five you're on the other side of the mountain, where the healing often begins.

This story has a sweet ending. A couple of months later, around the time of their 25th wedding anniversary, Pearl and her husband were visiting his parents. Pearl saw a marked change in Mom-in-law's communication with her. She was pleased to notice that neither a rash nor psoriasis had occurred. Then came the big gift, in the highest sense! Pearl was invited into the formal dining room where Mom-in-law was holding a beautiful, monogrammed sterling silver tray. She handed it to Pearl, saying "This tray was a gift for our wedding from Don's mother. We want you to have it with our love and best wishes for twenty-five more years." A shocker, a real shocker! Pearl emailed me the story about their weekend and the gift when she returned home. She thanked me for encouraging her to take the high road and let Love's Power loose on her life. Isn't Forgiveness amazing?!

A client's email about her family pattern

> Juliana… I'm having a problem with the completion letter to my Grandma. I read the directions on the Forgiveness Process, and the last part says something about forgiving them for

what we thought they caused, since we create what we experience. My issue is I was UNBORN … How could I have created that experience?? That doesn't make sense and makes me mad to think about it. I feel like she rejected me … she didn't want me … she has been nothing but abusive to my mom all these years. How can I as a baby create that? I mean … she HELPED create my negative feelings about myself. If she weren't such a bitch, I would never been born with those bad feelings about myself in the first place. How can I take responsibility for something she helped create, and say it was my fault when I was just developing?

In my family there has been this generational thing with the mother and the first-born daughter: the mothers are just very nasty and abusive to their first born daughters. My mom, even though we have our own issues, has tried to break this cycle. I'm unable to write this completion letter to my Grandma without getting mad. I am reasonable and can take responsibility where I feel I need to, but I just don't see what my responsibility in this is.
Thank you, Mary Ellen

Dear Mary Ellen,

First of all, none of this is "your fault." The idea that we create our experience has more to do with our choosing to buy into others' negative patterns,

THE OTHER F WORD

or not. We can choose in or choose out of them. Forgiveness is "letting go" and choosing NOT to be part of that pattern—choosing to be happy and to be free of that pattern. Your grandmother may continue to be that way for the rest of her life (since she was programmed that way), but you don't have to be part of her negative patterning. Step off one moving sidewalk onto another. That's all.

You are in charge of your mind. Free will, as it's called. You can choose to be angry with your grandmother, which puts you right in the same boat as her negativity, or you can choose to let her and her negative ways go. Bless her and let her go. Then you're free, Mary Ellen. And when you do that you are literally breaking the mother/first-born daughter generational pattern. That's huge! So by you seeing how negative this pattern is, and choosing to break it, you are doing something much bigger than only for yourself after you finish this forgiveness diet. Remember to pray for the words and determination before you write this letter.   Love, Juliana

An inherited grandmother pattern

Dana's father was just six years old when his father died, leaving his mother with four young children to raise by herself. This was the beginning of a lifetime of depression in Dana's grandmother's life, as well as a sad and melancholy childhood for her little family. Her own childhood had been hard for her grandmother, but this life was especially difficult for her. Having no help she had to depend on the children, including Dana's six-year-old father, to help with household chores. The children were expected to do small jobs for money to help the struggling family.

Dana's dad was never emotionally available to her. He would "plow ahead" and not deal with his emotions, maybe afraid of unleashing all the burdens he was holding inside. He and Dana's mom were never loving with each other, never even touching each other in front of the children. He worked hard ceaselessly; when he wasn't at work he was working hard at home. He never slowed down to feel or enjoy what was around him. His subconscious view of life had been taught to him by his mother: life is a struggle and it's hard. He was programmed with this thought, living it every day with everything he did.

As it goes in life, we pass on what we know to our children. Our children soak up the information, live it, pass it on to their children, and so on and so on. There are many traits worthwhile to be passed on, of course. But some may be left in the past, where they belong. All healing begins with recognition. We have to see the negative pattern in ourselves before we can choose to let it go or not. This struggle pattern of Dana's father was not serving him, nor did it serve Dana, as it was passed on to her.

Dana spent most of her life in depression. She felt she had some artistic ability but would never take time to give it expression. Her 26-year marriage was passionless and convenient. Counseling and sex therapy didn't help. Her husband's work was his life, and Dana was not part of it. She felt alienated from life, not having any idea of what joy felt like.

After doing the Forgiveness Process on herself, Dana began to shift. She began wearing colored clothing instead of always gray and black. She began fixing her hair and wearing lipstick. She began a painting class and took a yoga weekend workshop. These were fabulous expressions of her newfound freedom! But it was after she did the process on her father and grandmother that she began to glow. She was feeling joy for the first time in her life. Dana forgave her grandmother for innocently and unconsciously passing on the pattern of struggle and depression through her father to her. Dana chose to see her father, her grandmother and their lives differently as she chose an easier and lovely life for herself. Forgiveness did this for her, as it can do it for you.

ACTION: Light a candle for a relative who has died whom you have yet to forgive. Think of one thing that person did that you liked. Sit with that thought for one minute. Take a breath.

You are safe. You are innocent. You are loved.

"Divine Protection" by Juliana Ericson
www.JulianaEricson.com

The Truth About Me

Fear condemns people
*   and love forgives people.*
Forgiveness will unravel what my fear has produced.
Even if I cannot determine what it is I am afraid of,
I know that if I am judging, I am fearful.
Today I will remind myself that I am safe,
*   I am innocent*
*   and I am loved.*

– Juliana Ericson

"People are often unreasonable and self-centered.
Forgive them anyway.
If you are kind, people may accuse you of ulterior motives.
Be kind anyway.
If you are honest, people may cheat you.
Be honest anyway.
If you find happiness, people may be jealous.
Be happy anyway.
The good you do today may be forgotten tomorrow.
Do good anyway.
Give the world the best you have and it may never be enough.
Give your best anyway.
For you see, in the end, it is between you and God.
It was never between you and them anyway."

~ Mother Teresa

CHAPTER 12

How to Do the 7-Day Forgiveness Process

This powerful transformative process takes seven days to complete, longer if you wait to write the third part, the completion letter. The concept for this process is based on a biblical reference. When Jesus was asked how much to forgive, he answered seventy times seven (*Matt.* 18:21,22). I feel there is a reason these specific numbers are quoted. I have plenty of evidence that this process works!

If you are familiar with the 12-step programs you may see some similarities: recognizing there is a problem, admitting it, and apologizing for your part. You decide who you want to forgive first, although I suggest you begin with yourself, so you can feel the difference firsthand. You may choose to begin with the person who appears to be your biggest obstacle to your peace at this time in your life.

Just know that this first process is only the beginning. There will be more. Once you see how magnificently beautiful the changes are, I am confident you will be inspired to move on to your second, third and so on.

Repeats: I have actually done six Forgiveness Processes on myself over these seventeen years of my involvement in this work. The first was an overview. The ones that followed had to do with specific complaints, such as my money mismanagement, lack of mothering skills, poor choices in men, and so on. I've done five on my mother and three on my father. I am sure I will do more as time goes on. I continue to see my life's process uncovering more exciting opportunities for healing and expansion.

You will actually get to the point where you'll be grateful to people for angering you! They show you where you're holding and stuffing anger or resentment, where you're holding your personal growth back. You really can get to the point where you will say, "Thank you for helping me see my blind spot!" It saves years of additional work on yourself. You may find that your personal growth will take on a whole new maturity when you get to this point.

Part one, the angry letter

This process is in three parts. PART ONE consists of writing an angry letter to the person/archetype/concept/event you are angry about. Write from the first person : *I am furious with you about….* Write until you feel you have written it all out, knowing there is always more you can cover in another Forgiveness Process at a later time. I don't care if it takes ten pages—write, write, write! If it's hate you feel, say it. If you feel blame, say it. If it's disgust and resentment, say it! Bear in mind, this is NOT an enlightened letter. It will bring to the surface deep feelings you've been stuffing inside for gentle release. This is your chance to say what you have been holding in, possibly for a whole lifetime. There are no apologies or compassion here, only venom and anger, or anything else you're feeling.

Once you have written your angry letter, go to a place where you can be alone. Where no one can hear you, read the letter aloud. I say "aloud" because so often people feel they don't have the right to feel this anger, resentment or hurt. Your body has been holding these negative emotions in, now let your body physically feel it. Say it loud; feel it vibrate in your body. Speak from your power center/*dan tien*, if you can. (Your *dan tien* is in the area of your third chakra just below your waist.) Shout it if you want! Get that anger out of your body. Saying it out loud is very cathartic and healing.

Once you have read your angry letter and spewed out all those toxic emotions, then burn it. Now you're ready to heal that open wound with some holy neosporin®. :-) Be kind to yourself tonight; maybe a bubble bath or a walk in nature. I don't recommend going out to a party, or being around loud noises this first evening. There's an emotional rawness common at this point of the Forgiveness Process. Honor this time. Honor your physical and emotional body, and be gentle now. There will be time to celebrate soon enough!

Part Two: "70 times 7"

Part Two is the powerhouse of this whole process, although it's not effective without completing Part One first. As I have noted above, Jesus said "70 times 7." I have people write, seventy times for seven days, the following statement: *I [your name] now forgive you [the person's name] completely.* For the first twenty writings, you may choose to add *what* you want to forgive, such as *I Sally now forgive you Daddy for leaving Mom when I was seven.* It also helps if you use the name in reference to the age of what you're forgiving, such as "Daddy" if you're forgiving something he did when you were young. Also, use your childhood name, such as "Mikey" instead of "Mike," if you are forgiving an occurrence from your childhood.

As I have written in these stories, do not be surprised if you see something shift in your body/mind/spirit on Day Four. You are purging the poisons you have held in for so long, maybe a lifetime. Your body has made it a part of you, now you are literally tearing out a piece of yourself! But with this process, you're concurrently adding the medicine of Forgiveness as you create the wound.

Be courageous, and at the same time take care of yourself. I suggest you continue with your writing, unless your therapist or doctor feels otherwise. I am here to coach you, but you are ultimately in charge of your body, mind and spirit.

After finishing Part Two, take time to notice any little shifts or "miracles" you've experienced in the previous week that have to do with the relationship you're working on. (For example, if you are doing your Forgiveness Process on an overbearing mother, you may have noticed mother-aged women or women with your mom's characteristics giving you unexpected compliments or unrequested respect. For example, if you're doing one on men, because you may have always chosen boyfriends who mistreated or devalued you, you might experience men being kind to you. I'm just asking you to notice, even the small things. As you see these shifts, you'll notice more and more unimaginable changes. They are ALL your creations! You choose to change your life by changing your thinking. Imagine what more you can do!

Part three, the completion letter

If you do not feel like this is easy to write on Day Seven, then wait another day or two. I actually waited six extra days before writing the completion letter on my third sister. Don't wait too long, though; you're creating alchemy here. Do not let it cool down. Even if you aren't feeling completely cleared of your anger, write this completion letter anyway. You *will* see a shift. (You'll probably want to do another Forgiveness Process later to clear things up with a person you resist completing.)

In the final step of this Forgiveness Process, think back to what you were angriest about with this person. What part did you play? What did you learn from the experience? We are never a victim. In thinking you were a victim, you gave your power away, but with this letter you can take that power back. What's the difference between the CEO and the janitor of a company? The thoughts they think. The CEO thinks "I can"; the janitor thinks "I can't!" This is your opportunity to change your thoughts and change your life.

This completion letter only needs to be a couple of paragraphs, not long like the first one. You are crystallizing the essence of this precious gift to yourself. Now you're going to bring this Forgiveness Process full-circle and complete it. You are going to mail it. You don't have to actually mail it to the person you are forgiving for the completion energy to be activated. If you choose to, just mail it like this: Put your letter in an envelope with **no return address**. Write the person's first name only and the city, but **with no street address**. Put a stamp on it. Drop it in the post office box, after you seal it with a kiss. Let it go.

Why never to do simultaneous forgiveness processes

An over-achiever client of mine caused herself some undue stress while doing her Forgiveness Process. Rena did not want to wait to finish one before she began another. I never, repeat *never*, suggest doing two Processes simultaneously. Here is why:

Successful, talented, beautiful, powerful, smart. She had it all. Honestly, I was a little intimidated by Rena. Two years before our first meeting, she had divorced, after twelve years in an abusive marriage. One year later, she'd decided to go out on her own in the design field. She'd had one successful opportunity after another. Rena was on a fast track to something wonderful. Her assertiveness, perseverance and savvy were paying off. A week before she came to see me for a session she had connected with a high-end international catalog company. She and her lawyer would be looking over contracts for the deal by the next week. Wow!

Doing the Forgiveness Process on oneself first seems to be helpful in getting people on the Forgiveness track, so on her second session I suggested it to Rena. She noticed some wonderful shifts in her life and her mind after finishing, and she wanted to do another one. I felt it would help her to move through the intense anger she held for her mother who had belittled and berated her so terribly as a child, so she did that one next. This Process on her mother was difficult for her, making Rena physically sick for the first few days. She had trouble sleeping and was irritable at work. Then on the sixth day, even with the process on her mother still incomplete, she felt the need to do a Forgiveness Process on her ex-husband, and wrote her angry letter. Note that since she had not finished the process on her mother, this was like two freight trains colliding.

Rena went into a tailspin as she found out that two essential components of her designs had been discontinued. They were very unique, and she did not know where to find another vendor at this late notice. Without all the important elements in place, her international deal would not happen. She sank right into feeling worthless and a failure.

I believe that what had happened was twofold: One, the hateful and bitter energy towards her ex-husband was moving out of her body after all these years. At the same time, the energy she was releasing from ending her mother's Forgiveness Process was colliding with the angry energy at the beginning of her ex-husband's Forgiveness Process. Train wreck!

Not only do I not discourage people from doing two Forgiveness Processes simultaneously, I don't even want people doing them back-to-back. I suggest leaving at least a few days in between them. There can be some large shifts in the emotional and mental bodies that need time to settle in. Taking time also allows you to recognize and reflect on the shifts in your life you will see that are created by this fabulous process. I especially love to see the many tiny miracles, shifts and changes in my life after doing a Forgiveness Process. I liken it to finding fairy dust spread all over my life!

ACTION: Choose who you want to forgive first (suggestion: yourself) and begin your Forgiveness Process. Look into your eyes in a mirror daily for a week and say *I love you (your name)*.

You are safe. You are innocent. You are loved.

"Beautiful" by Juliana Ericson
www.JulianaNashville.com

Now

As I forgive others
I realize that the person I need to forgive most is myself.
I have been blaming others for what I thought they did to me
        because I have allowed myself to feel
                insignificant and unworthy.
I have not recognized the beauty that I really am
        and the love inside me is waiting
                to be released and shared.
I have been hiding my light
        and blaming others for how bad I have felt.
Today my eyes are open
        and I am no longer willing to live in that dark place.
I will forgive everyone for everything I thought they did to me.
        I will begin today.
                I will begin now.

– Juliana Ericson

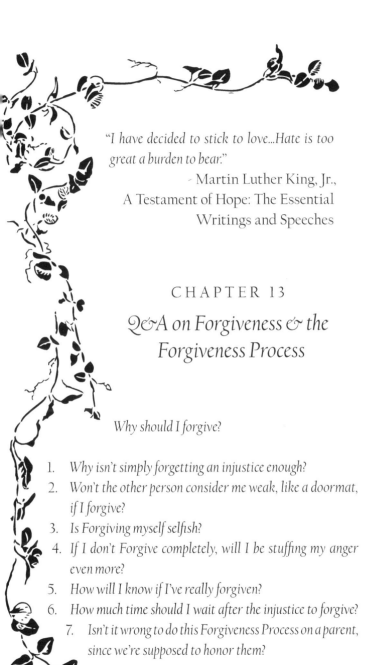

"I have decided to stick to love...Hate is too great a burden to bear."
- Martin Luther King, Jr.,
A Testament of Hope: The Essential Writings and Speeches

CHAPTER 13

Q&A on Forgiveness & the Forgiveness Process

Why should I forgive?

1. Why isn't simply forgetting an injustice enough?
2. Won't the other person consider me weak, like a doormat, if I forgive?
3. Is Forgiving myself selfish?
4. If I don't Forgive completely, will I be stuffing my anger even more?
5. How will I know if I've really forgiven?
6. How much time should I wait after the injustice to forgive?
7. Isn't it wrong to do this Forgiveness Process on a parent, since we're supposed to honor them?

8. *Can I also forgive other things, places, organizations, groups?*

9. *How many times can I forgive the same person?*

10. *What is the difference between Forgiveness and justice?*

11. *Who should I Forgive first in the sequence?*

12. *Why do I have to write the process? Why can't I just think about it or speak the process?*

13. *What if I miss a day of writing the seven day process?*

14. *Why does the process have those 3 specific parts? What is the significance of each?*

15. *How long will it take until I feel the peace you're talking about in this book?*

1. *Why should I forgive?* First and foremost, we are doing the Forgiving as a gift to ourselves; it is not for the other person. Our bodies and minds, our lives and futures benefit when we are present. Being present is really living. It's impossible to be present when we're carrying grudges from the past. When we allow negative feelings toward someone or something to take over, then our mind can become consumed with a sense of injustice and bitterness. As we do this, we live the old injustice over and over, reliving the pain over and over again. It's as if we are flogging ourselves repeatedly, while blaming someone else for hurting us.

It is common to bring old anger and bitterness into current relationships, making them difficult and emotionally heavy. We are then merely existing, not actually living, as we hold on to such toxins as pain, anger and resentments from the past. They poison our joy, our relationships. They poison the full and best experience of life we could be having. We can only know the depth of intimate relationships when we finally let down our defenses and allow ourselves to be vulnerable. This type of intimacy is what creates solid and authentic loving relationships.

Another reason to forgive is that it is a huge drain on our health. According to The Mayo Clinic, forgiveness can improve health in the following ways:

> Lessening anxiety, stress and hostility
> Lowering blood pressure
> Creating fewer symptoms of depression
> Producing greater psychological well-being
> Lowering the risk of alcohol and substance abuse

Failure to address these factors can also lead to heart disease, and other health challenges.

Our livers break down toxic and unusable substances in the blood, forming usable compounds for the body. In Qigong Chinese medicine it is believed that the liver does the same for the flow of energy. Signs of blocked or stagnated liver energy include: depression, anger, fatigue, stress and moodiness. Qigong professionals believe that our anger tends to be stored in the liver. (I have often wondered if there's a connection between people who have cirrhosis of the liver and unforgiveness).

2. *Why isn't simply forgetting an injustice enough?* When we forget but don't forgive we are simply stuffing our anger deeper inside us, like trying to stuff an elephant into a hat! The anger is not gone just because we're not consciously thinking of it daily. Our resentment can often emerge in unexplainable bursts of anger: in depression, sadness, confusion and the inability to be intimate. It also comes out in projection, where we project our anger onto an innocent person who may only have similar characteristics or mannerisms as the person with whom we are angry.

Taking a neutral stance on the person who has wronged us probably indicates that we are stuffing it and do not want to deal with the issue. "*Oh, Mary always reacts that way. She doesn't mean anything by it.*" is really denying that you have been hurt by what was done to you. You deserve to feel your feelings. You can acknowledge them, then let them go with a Forgiveness Process. Acknowledging the suffering you have felt is loving yourself enough to say it (in the Part I anger letter), and attribute the responsibility for the unkind words or actions to the wrongdoer.

When you do not acknowledge the wrongdoer's injustice, as in the example above with Mary, it may also deny the value of the other person. It's as though you are saying, "*It doesn't matter why she said it, it's not worth my time or attention to bother with it.*"

THE OTHER F WORD

3. *Won't the other person consider me weak, like a doormat, if I forgive?* To forgive is a very courageous act. It is weaker to push anger inside of you without dealing with it for years. Remember that you are doing this process for yourself, NOT the other person. You will be the one who leads a fuller, happier life, whether the wrongdoer does or not. To forgive is an act of strength because you are willing to give up the struggle, which is courageous.

> *"The weak can never forgive. Forgiveness is the attribute of the strong."* - Mahatma Gandhi

4. *Is Forgiving myself selfish?* It is selfish for you *not* to forgive, holding your best self inside you. It is a gift to your family, friends, and community to be your full self. You cannot be your best self when you carry around anger-baggage from the past. I suggest if you are feeling guilty for forgiving yourself that you take time to be patient and loving with yourself, acknowledging that deep inside you are hurting.

5. *If I don't Forgive completely, will I be stuffing my anger even more?* Any movement you make toward reconciliation is a step in the right direction. There is freedom for your soul with any anger released, any resentment calmed. I believe that any amount of anger and resentment we release is excellent progress. Life is a process which is never

finished. If we do not eliminate all of our anger in one Forgiveness Process, we have the option to do more. There is no limit to how much we can forgive a person. I have seen that once people see how much better their lives are, they want to do more of these transformative Forgiveness Processes. You can also.

6. *How will I know if I've truly forgiven?* You will know you have really forgiven when you see or even think about that person. You'll not feel the same knot in your stomach, the same old desire for revenge, the same dark hopelessness. You'll also notice that you have stopped meeting people who have the same negative character traits as that person. Once you have really forgiven, your subconscious will no longer have the need to attract circumstances or people to remind you about forgiving the original person. This is one of the blessings of Forgiveness most people fail to mention, and it's actually one of my favorite parts!

7. *How much time after the injustice should I wait to forgive?* It depends on the injustice and how you are feeling. Some wrongdoings require time to process and work through. Others can be done quickly and will require little effort, with confidence that the reward will be huge. There are no hard and fast rules about when to begin, except that Forgiveness is a choice. It is important to feel the anger, if you have access to it, and express it appropriately. This

is part of the healing process, and is an integral part of the particular Forgiveness process in this book. If you do not acknowledge your negative feelings in the anger letter they will surface at other times. Use this opportunity to allow what is inside you to surface for healing and release. You will feel much better!

8. *Isn't it sinful to do this Forgiveness Process on a parent, since we're supposed to honor them?* The Fifth Commandment, "Honor your mother and father," is actually enhanced and realized with this Forgiveness process. Many, many clients of mine had had terrible relationships with their parents before doing this Forgiveness Process. Afterward, they were able to have honest and authentic conversations with their parents. They could enjoy their parents' company and understand that we can honor our parents without having to condone their bad behavior or repeat negative parental patterns. All healing begins with recognition, and Forgiveness is the natural healing choice to follow.

9. *Can I also forgive other things, places, organizations, groups?* I have had great success with forgiving places, things, cultures and even concepts. I've had success personally, as well as with my clients. The idea is that we create an archetype of the negative thought pattern and focus our Forgiveness on that. For example, many people

have felt that money is bad, that it's caused greed, wars, family break ups, etc. So I have some clients do the process on money, even writing their letter to "Dear money." All of their anger comes out in these angry letters, just as for people. Our subconscious thoughts want to blame someone for how badly we feel, so it doesn't matter if we are blaming a person, a place, thing or a concept. It still works. Examples of non-human subjects for Forgiveness Processes I have seen are: money, sex, political parties, governments, cultures, religions and corporations.

If you are angry, for instance, at an institution try first forgiving the person there whom you find especially infuriating. That might be the core of your anger instead of the institution itself.

10. *How many times can I forgive the same person?* I feel that there's no limit. I personally have forgiven my father three times, my mother five times and myself six times. Each time was for something different. For example, the first time I forgave myself it was as an overall Forgiveness, which included some details, but mainly it was general Forgiveness. A year or so later, I forgave myself for making poor choices in boyfriends over the years. Another time I forgave myself for squandering a great deal of money in my past. So each time you can forgive something specific, or for the same thing if you feel a particular issue still needs more letting-go work.

11. *What is the difference between Forgiveness and justice?* When we Forgive it is a personal and moral response to the wrongdoing. Justice, on the other hand, is a community and civic response to a wrongdoing. Justice can dictate the outcome of the wrongdoing. We must dictate the outcome of our own feelings about the wrongdoing. Our response in Forgiveness is separate from justice, as it is our personal choice.

I have seen people hold resentment against a person even after justice had already been done. They were not willing for that to suffice. They felt the need to hold anger against that person, maybe thinking anger would make them suffer more. Anger against that person was hurting the person holding the anger much more than the recipient. A great example of this is in the true story "Dead Man Walking." In the movie, a couple is horrendously tortured and killed. One of the men who committed the crime is on death row. He is regularly visited by a nun wanting to help him confess to her so he might release guilt before he dies, having some peace at his death. The family of one of the victims is in shambles because of hatred and revenge. They're fighting among themselves. Revenge and anger has sucked the life out of them until they have become mere shells of people. One of the family-members asks the nun how the man could find peace in the midst of all of the brokenness. She teaches him that the only way he can survive it is for him to forgive the murderers. Otherwise he will continue to feel like a dead man, which he had told the nun was his feeling.

12. *Who should I forgive first in the sequence?* There are several main Forgiveness processes I recommend to do at least once: ourself, mother, father, siblings, God/Religion and our Obstetrician (our first authority figure). I think the Process benefits people greatly when they forgive themselves first. They can see for themselves the breadth of change that is possible. It also improves their joy-and-happiness quotient immediately, giving hope for a new and different future. After that, I suggest doing the Process on the person you are seeing evidence for in your life at that point in time. For instance, if you had a bossy, overbearing mother, you might experience people bossing you a lot for a month or two. That would show me your desire to heal and renew your relationship with your mother, by subconsciously attracting bossy people to you. Patterns such as this are very helpful to show us what path to follow in many of life's quandaries. Remember: Our life is a mirrored reflection of our thoughts, both conscious *and* subconscious.

13. *Why do I have to write the process? Why can't I simply think about it?* There is a certain power when we get our bodies involved in the Forgiveness. We can literally rewire our brains by creating NEW

neuropathways. In the cutting-edge science Neurogenesis (new brain cell development), researchers have found in a number of test subjects that neurons are continuously being formed, even by the elderly! Behavior also has a significant impact on how many new cells are grown, so now we know you CAN teach an old dog new tricks! Many other studies have shown that changes take place deeper & more rapidly when the mind and body are used in tandem when learning desired changes.

14. *What if I miss a day of writing the seven day writing process?* I have two answers to this question. My first answer is directed toward an easier Forgiveness process. If you miss a day, or even two, of a fairly "easy" Forgiveness process, my thought is to go ahead and continue. If you miss a day of a difficult one, maybe on a person you have put off for years, I say begin again at the beginning. Your resistance is going to pull out some deeper anger for you. I have had people begin three, four, even five times! If you find it too difficult, get support from a friend or a coach. (You may schedule an appointment with me at www.breathworks.net, my Life Coaching website.)

15. *Why does the process have those 3 specific parts? What is the significance of each?* The three parts are essential to the success of your Forgiveness work. As I have mentioned, we have to feel our anger before we can

release it; otherwise, it is merely a philosophical exercise. Allowing ourselves to feel the anger is honoring our past selves *with* the pain and our future selves *without* it.

In Part Two we are applying what I call a "spiritual Neosporin®" with the positive statements. Once we have torn open our hearts by writing the anger letter, we have to fill the wound with healing balm: Forgiveness. Meanwhile, the number of times we write is based on a Biblical reference: when Jesus was asked how many times to forgive he said "70 times 7." This number is considered by many to represent spiritual perfection.

Part Three is essential because it is a closure for the entire process. The last part of any sacred process is as essential as the beginning and middle. All three parts create the complete successful work. It is important for us to see the blessing we received from the anger we originally had. If we don't see the blessing then it's possible that we will continue to see ourselves as victim, which is not true. We are never a victim; there's always a choice, whether the choices are all pleasurable or not. The blessing could be as simple as, "*I now recognize what traits I do want to have as a parent for my children, by learning what traits I do not want to have.*"

16. *How long will it take until I feel the peace you're talking about in this book?* Life is an ongoing process. We are never "done." I suggest you begin with your

first Forgiveness Process, the one on yourself. You will start to see the brilliance of life without blame and anger, without bringing past hurt into the present. You'll know what it is like to be in the present. You'll begin to see life with new eyes, with innocence. Then you'll know the peace I am talking about. You'll know that it is all good: life is about feeling, living and loving.

ACTION: Make a list of ten people from your past you would like to Forgive. Name your reason for forgiving each one. After Forgiving the main six mentioned in this chapter, begin on these ten people (even if it takes a year).

You are safe. You are innocent. You are loved.

nothing here's real
and everyone's alike

by Nila Frederiksen

Something I Know For Sure

I know
that when I inwardly bless people
at the time they make me angry
it is likely I won't allow that temporary anger
to settle into my body.
I understand what toxic negative emotions do
to the health of my body
and I choose to let them go in the moment
whenever I can.
If I feel I need help to do that
I call on my guide, God, to help me.
I am sure
that with God
all things
are possible.

– Juliana Ericson

"Let no man pull you so low as to hate him."
- Martin Luther King, Jr., A Knock
at Midnight: Inspiration from
the Great Sermons of Reverend
Martin Luther King, Jr.

CHAPTER 14

Physical Healing and Forgiveness

Often Physical Illness can originate from a thought or a feeling. Some common examples include: an ulcer and high blood pressure stemming from anger, fear or overwhelm; hives and insomnia brought on by the presence of intense or ongoing fear; anorexia due to self-rejection; and heart attack from lack of joy. In Louise L. Hay's book, *You Can Heal Your Life*, she states that there are really only two main mental patterns that contribute to our creation of disease: fear and anger. In her book she lists almost 50 pages of illnesses with their probable mental causes and suggested new thought patterns.

For instance, with regard to lower back pain, she cites "Fear of money. Lack of financial support." Then as a replacement thought pattern she suggests using the positive thoughts: "I trust the process of life. All I need is always taken care of. I am safe." For breast problems she writes: "Failure to nourish oneself. Putting everyone else first." She suggests replacing those negative thoughts with: "I'm important. I count. I now care for and nourish myself with joy. I allow others the freedom to be who they are" to help the healing. (My sister Carla, who was diagnosed with breast cancer several years ago, is now cancer-free, while learning the joy of nourishing herself.)

Of course there is more to healing than simply thinking positive affirmations. There is even more than taking the right medicine or undergoing the prescribed surgery. I am sure you've heard of people getting a clean bill of health from their doctor after a surgery, only to return with the same illness or a similar one. Why do you think that is so? Could it be that their bodies have not healed the core thought that might have caused the illness in the first place? If a woman has carpal tunnel syndrome but has not forgiven her anger and frustration at life's seeming injustices (*You Can Heal Your Life, pg. 186*), there's a good chance her problem may re-occur even after surgery.

We are not only physical beings, we are multi-faceted beings. Let's take into account our mental and emotional well-being as we examine our physical health. Of the two main reasons that may be contributing to our creation of disease, fear and anger, both are within our choice. Forgiveness, a change of heart as it's been called, releases anger, helping us see that fear is unnecessary. So it is a win/win project. Even if it does not improve your physical condition, Forgiveness will greatly improve your quality of life, which might in its own right be worth it all. Forgiveness is essential to a full life and to life itself.

People who are willing to forgive are generally less anxious and stressed; they also enjoy better cardiovascular health, lower blood pressure and a renewed physical energy inspired by the hope and optimism derived from their forgiveness work.

Healing beyond the physical body

When Ellen came to me, it was mainly to see if I could help her with her sight. She was 63 and quickly becoming blind due to macular degeneration. She had been legally blind for a few years and on disability. Her husband had died the previous year and she was worried that as her eyesight was becoming increasingly worse she would have to go into an assisted living home prematurely.

Even though that was reason enough for her to be fearful, that was not Ellen's biggest hurdle to peace. Blame was. She blamed others A LOT for her lack of happiness. She has done this most of her life after learning the pattern from her mother (who had learned it from her mother). Ellen's lack of money was her late husband's fault. Her increased weight gain was her father's fault. Her being late was the traffic's fault. Her lack of friends was her sister's fault. It was always someone else's fault, and never her own.

In Ellen's first session I helped her see where she was not taking responsibility for her life. She agreed to notice when she was blaming others and change her thoughts in the moment. She also agreed to begin giving herself what she felt she was lacking: acknowledgment and support. Ellen's affirmations that week were "I am now willing to see my own beauty and magnificence" and "I accept Divine Guidance and am always safe."

The next week she did a Forgiveness Process on her father, who had been absent from his wife and children during most of Ellen's childhood. He had stayed away from the house as much as possible, out with the guys, not wanting to be part of his family's chaos that he was aware he was causing. He had not helped with his children's upbringing, leaving it entirely to his overburdened and overwhelmed wife. He'd made very little money, so the small salary had only kept his family of five children in poverty. Ellen's childhood had been one of complete disorder and uncertainty. She blamed her father. Her main thought about life was "Life is a struggle," and her whole life had reflected that core belief.

The next session she agreed to forgive her mother for giving power away so easily to a man who did not honor her or the family. Ellen's mother had been angry and bitter, and had had no friends. As a result of her failed relationship with her husband, Ellen's mother had manipulated the children with guilt, by threatening to hurt herself or leave them. She had also kept their house so messy and dirty that Ellen was embarrassed to have friends over, so she had few friends all through her school years. This week was Ellen's turning point.

She suddenly began to see her face a little more clearly in the mirror without her glasses. She was amazed! What is even more exciting was all of the new support she was receiving from her family and helpful strangers she encountered. Before the Forgiveness work, her sister had been repelled and drained by Ellen's neediness, rarely contacting her. When she began to notice a marked improvement in Ellen's voice, her sister began telephoning twice a week! Ellen's brother, Joe, also called her for the first time in a year and half.

She began meeting new friends in the public van for handicapped persons. She learned about a whole new network of opportunities for blind people she'd had no idea existed! Her life was opening up with fun and excitement for the first time in many, many years! Although her physical eyesight was improving only minimally, her "emotional sight" had improved dramatically. She was seeing a new truth: that life CAN be easy, and it CAN support you.

In addition, her mother was actually now making friends in the nursing home. She began writing notes and calling family, something she had not done in sixty years. Ellen's Forgiveness Process completion letter had released her mother, from the guilt she had carried for so long. As Ellen let go of her life-long resentments, the family was opening up!

Marie and her STD

She was 22 years old, beautiful and full of joyous intensity. Marie was one of those people who really does live life to the max in every moment. She loved big; she shared big; she dreamed big . . . and then she hit a big wall. This was when I first met her. She had been referred to me by a friend after having what she called "an emotional meltdown."

Marie was in Nashville to fulfill her dream of becoming a Country singer/songwriter. She had had a burning desire to sing professionally since childhood. She was singing with a band, writing music three days a week and having a ball in Music City. Marie's life was on track and she was enjoying every minute of it! Then she met Dean at a party. He was drop-dead gorgeous, fun and wealthy. Marie was hooked. They talked and laughed for hours that night at the party, then agreed to see each other the following weekend.

After a classic movie at the Belcourt Theatre, they walked arm-in-arm under the moonlight around Centennial Park. She was falling for this guy, and fast! When he took her home, she agreed to let him come into her apartment for a few minutes. One thing led to another and then they were kissing passionately on her couch. After a few minutes, Dean began pulling off her clothes. She pushed him away. "No! I'm saving myself!" But the harder she struggled the more aggressive he became. She screamed, but no one heard. Then it was over. Dean saw the blood and realized that, as Marie had said, she had been a virgin. He walked out the door without looking back. She was angry, humiliated, fearful and ashamed. Was it her fault? Had she led him on? It was all too much for her to bear. She became depressed.

That had been two years prior to her session with me. In the meantime she'd found that Dean had transmitted genital herpes to her. It had complicated her intimate life, but she was managing her herpes with medication from a doctor. The worst part of the herpes was the anger: anger at Dean, anger at the herpes, anger at herself. It had become overwhelming for Marie to cope. That was when she found me and this work.

I learned she had two older sisters whose promiscuity had embarrassed her as a child. One night in particular Marie's teenage sisters had thrown a party while their parents were out of town. Lots of teenagers, lots of liquor, lots of sex. And 8-year old Marie had seen more than she wished she had. While under the kitchen table and out of sight, she's seen one boy pushing and mistreating Marie's sister. He'd had sex with her while she was too drunk to notice her younger sister watching the whole thing.

Marie cried as she recalled that night, "I remember right then and there I made a promise to myself: I would never dishonor myself or my body like that. I would save myself for my husband. But then Dean did the same thing to me!"

I took out my copy of Louise Hay's book and read what it said about herpes: "*Mass belief in sexual guilt and the need for punishment. Public shame. Belief in a punishing God.*" That was it! Marie had the subconscious thought that sex was bad, and that her sister was guilty and needed to be punished. Her years in Catholic School had ingrained in her the idea that sex before marriage was a sin. Then when she was raped *she* felt guilty and felt the need to be punished.

In the following months I had Marie do Forgiveness Processes on Dean, herself, her sister, sex and the Catholic

Church, because of the anger she felt against all of them. Her herpes outbreaks lessened to the point that she went six months without any. Then it was longer and longer. Lately, Marie even had a blood test to prove to herself she was clean. She is. She let go of guilt, shame, judgment and anger. Forgiveness can do these things.

A lifetime of emotional pain held in his shoulder

Barry was passionate about his music. He practiced his violin every day for hours, always had. Violin playing had been his whole life from the time he was nine years old. To him there was nothing beyond his violin and his music. He was willing to give up everything for his art. When other boys played sports, he was working on a tough Dmitri Shostakovich piece. When he had spare weekends, Barry was polishing up his version of Bach Brandenburg Concertos. His goal was to be a professional violinist in a great symphony. After graduating with honors from The Julliard School, he felt empowered to name his orchestra and his price.

Barry had then auditioned for a couple of symphonies and performed brilliantly. He'd been offered positions in both. What an honor! He'd been simply elated! The symphony closer to his home and family had suited him best. He'd wanted to be able to drive home on weekends. All the years of practicing and sacrificing were finally being paid back. Or so he'd thought.

It was only the second week of practice with his new symphony position when Barry had noticed his shoulder more sore than normal after only a three-hour rehearsal. He'd gone home and massaged some analgesic balm on his shoulder, which usually did the trick to relieve his occasional soreness. But this had been different: His shoulder was even sorer when he awoke the next morning. It was so bad that he'd been unable to even lift his arm to brush his teeth. "This is not good" he thought. Only three weeks into the schedule and he already had such an intense reaction. The amount of violin playing Barry was doing with the symphony was not excessive for him; it was no more hours a day than he had played since he'd been a child. His muscles and joints were used to this. What was wrong?

After trying to heal himself with doctors, therapists, chiropractors, acupuncturists and alternative healers, he had made the painful decision to quit the symphony. He simply could not play. The pain was too intense. As you can imagine, this had thrown Barry into quite a depression. He would not leave his apartment and had no desire to even eat. He didn't go home for weeks, because he was too ashamed of what had become of his illustrious career and talent.

He'd finally pulled himself together and gotten a job at a university library. He'd just stuffed himself into a cubicle and vegetated there. Barry's life had become gray and lifeless. He never told his co-workers about his violin or his passion. It had been too painful to bring it up.

Barry heard about my work through a physical therapist he was seeing for his shoulder. He felt compelled to try my method of healing past emotional wounds. He could not go on living such a shallow existence. There had to be another way, he thought.

In our first session, I learned about his love of the violin and what had happened to that love. I also learned about his birth and prenatal experience, and found out that Barry had been delivered with forceps, which had made his birth an extremely painful one.

It is very common for forceps-birthed people to sabotage their successes. Success is the end of a process, and so is birth. They mix these thoughts together at a very deep subconscious level, creating the belief that endings are painful. They will sabotage successes before they are completed, so they will not have to feel the pain they expect will happen at the end of the situation.

The good news is that all healing begins with recognition. When I showed him this pattern, Barry was amazed and began to recollect many more examples of sabotage in his life. In addition to working with affirmations that turned his pre-verbal negative program around, I had him do a Forgiveness Process on his OB/GYN, the doctor who had delivered him with the forceps in the first place. (Even though forceps delivery is usually mandated when necessary and even life-saving, it still is very painful to the baby.) I wanted Barry to do all he could to try to turn his life around, and to bring the love of his life back in.

His shoulder healed. It was gradual, but Barry eventually began teaching violin to private students. For his whole life, he had been used to playing beautifully, and only exactly what was written. Then some friends asked if he wanted to start jamming with them in one of their basements. He had never done free-form playing before; he had always played only the notes on the music sheets. This was another landscape for him: Freedom! He was enjoying it. He was really, really enjoying it!

I got an email from Barry recently with the time and date of his next musical engagement. He's part of a progressive jazz group here in Nashville. They have a great style and a loyal following. It's really different from the Rachmaninoff and Haydn he used to play. He's having a ball, doing what he loves. Who would have thought that forgiving his doctor for the forceps birth would lead Barry to this joyous result?

ACTION: Do you have an illness that you might affect by doing a Forgiveness Process on a certain person or thing in your life? How about trying?

You are safe. You are innocent. You are loved.

"Safe" by Juliana Ericson
www.JulianaNashville.com

One Precious Thing

I want one thing, and one thing only.
I want to be happy.
For me to be happy
    I know I need to release my anger and judgments,
        which keep me imprisoned.
I can't be happy when I am mentally attacking others.
I can't be happy when I resent and blame others.
I can't be happy when I feel a victim
    because of what I believe others have done to me.
When I feel victimized I have to defend myself,
    and I cannot feel safe that way.
I want one thing, and one thing only.
I want to be happy.

– Juliana Ericson

"With Forgiveness, expect miracles!"
- Juliana Ericson

CHAPTER 15

Prosperity Released Through Forgiveness

Have you ever wondered why you only make a certain amount of money, and cannot seem to increase your salary no matter how you try? It might surprise you that most people subconsciously set their own limit on how much money they can make. We tend to set our financial ceiling at about the same level as the breadwinner's salary in the family of our youth. Sounds crazy, but it is true.

Try it now. In today's dollars, how much did your mom or dad make when you were growing up? How does that compare to your salary? If it's close to the same amount and you want to make more, you can make a choice to break that pattern using this Forgiveness Process. If it's much higher, what are your feelings about the difference in

189

dollar amount? Do you feel guilty that you make more? Or are you overcompensating, trying to prove something to someone? If it's much lower, is it difficult for you to see yourself as an adult who could make more than your parent did? These are some questions to shake things up and help you delve into your prosperity hiding-place. It would be worth some of your time to really look at your subconscious thoughts about money, wealth and wealthy people.

Inheriting financial patterns from our parents

I had Darren look at his subconscious thoughts about money, wealth and his family patterns. He was burdened and angry with his job and felt trapped. He wanted his work to be purposeful, but it was not. He felt that to provide for his family he had to put his passion on hold, believing it could not provide enough money for his family to maintain their desired standard of living. He loved working out, had a great physique and wanted to be a personal trainer who could help people stay fit and healthy. He tried this for a while on a part-time basis, but it didn't work out. He felt he did not succeed because he lacked the credentials he felt he needed. In the meantime, he was working at a big-box home improvement store, hating every minute of it.

In his sessions with me I learned that he came from hard-working, blue-collar parents who had not graduated from high school. Life and money had always been a struggle. When he was six years old, he had realized that his family was poor when he heard kids making fun of his old running shoes. He remembered having the thought, "I'll never have what I want, because I'm not worthy." His father had called him stupid, even though he had worked hard and made good grades. He heard "We can't afford it!" so often that he had never even asked his parents for what he wanted, since he knew the answer. It is often at this point in life where people often make the subconscious decision: "I can make it!" or "I can't make it!" Darren had decided, "I can't make it!" and had lived his life that way: as a struggle.

During those years Darren had also made the subconscious decisions "money is bad" and "wealthy people are bad." Both of these thoughts had kept him from having what he wanted. His ideas about money and wealthy people were so negative that he didn't want to be associated with either. He had subconsciously associated with his father's beliefs: "I'm not worthy" and "you have to work hard to get money." Even though Darren was handsome and intelligent, he'd stayed in his struggle pattern with little money for years.

The first Forgiveness Process I had him do was on himself. Darren had several issues to work through and I wanted him to see his own worth first. His first shift was that he stopped allowing himself to be manipulated by guilt. He stopped feeling guilty with his own judgments, as well as when others used the guilt-card against him. He said "I almost feel guilty for not feeling guilty!" This was a breakthrough, because this guilt about being educated and becoming successful, when his father had been neither, was what had kept him broke.

The next process was on his father. They had always loved each other, that was not the issue. Darren was clear that he had to release the blame against his father for the constant struggle he had experienced in his life. He wanted to release the bond to his father's pattern of giving up and feeling unworthy. He knew he had to create a new pattern, one that served him and his children. He was excited to see how his life could become different.

His son was the first to notice that Darren had stopped fighting with his wife about money as they used to, and as Darren's parents had done before him. Then he began feeling a shift in his thoughts about working hard, about hating his job. He could feel a shift in his body that life could be easier, that he could actually make money doing what he enjoyed. This was huge! He was now able to imagine what an easier life would be like, an important step in the prosperity process he had not been able to experience before.

In the last of this prosperity sequence of Forgiveness processes, I had Darren work on forgiving money itself. He still had thoughts of it being bad, that only worthy people had money, and that money was the "root of evil." It's easy to understand that these thoughts had to be unearthed and transformed before he could become successful!

In the months that followed, Darren's relationship with his parents improved dramatically. Now that his guilt and blaming of his father were gone, he was able to be more present with them. He began night classes to become a personal trainer. He wanted to have a fulfilling career and was determined to finish.

I heard from Darren recently. He is no longer dreading

his work at the home improvement store; he quit. He is now a happy and prosperous small business owner. He has a successful full-time personal training business with many high-profile clients. He's in the midst of creating a training video with an investor and has a great investment portfolio. Who would believe this was the same man from two years ago!

Diamonds emerging from the muck

For as long as he could remember, George had had anger issues with his mother. She had always been the bread-winner, while his dad had overspent and run up tons of credit-card debt. His financial patterns had followed his father's lead. Within months of graduating from college and being out on his own, he was running up debt on his new credit cards. "I just kept shopping and shopping, whether I needed it or not." he explained. Before long he had gotten in over his head. By the time he came to see me he had created a successful business and was making good money, but his high living was way more than he could afford.

He decided he needed extra funds. A few years prior to our first session, George's father had filed bankruptcy, while his mother had become a self-made millionaire. He'd called his mother for a loan. She agreed. After that, the calls had become more and more frequent. His mother would become increasingly resentful and reluctant to loan her seemingly successful son money. This pattern was exactly the same as his parents' money pattern had been. Mom had made the money, and Dad had overspent. Mom had gotten angry and resentful with Dad and was now repeating the same with her son.

Before I had him begin the Forgiveness Process on his mother, I had George do some work on the financial pattern he had subconsciously copied from his over-spending father. Simply recognizing the pattern he had taken on helped slow it down; then came some affirmation work, along with another letting-go process of some patterns. Now he was ready to do the Forgiveness Process on his mother, who in his eyes had never thought he was good enough.

By the fourth day of this Forgiveness Process, he was in such a place of self-pity he could hardly work. His sales were down. "It was awful! I didn't want to do anything!" George admitted. He texted me, asking if it was normal for him to feel that way. I reminded him about the dips that sometime happens on Day Four, and assured him that he'd get through it. By the fifth day he felt a little better, but was still weak and sad. Day Six revealed to him how his mother had been in charge of his whole life, and how he had *given* that charge to her. He began to feel good enough to take his power back. He also began to really feel that he deserved better, and deserved to experience his own power. He was no longer feeling resentment toward his mother about this issue, because he now saw that he had been the one creating it all.

Within a week his sales went up 19 percent. The following week they were up 22 percent. It was no accident that these numbers rose. Forgiveness affects all parts of our lives, including our prosperity.

ACTION:

- List ten beliefs you have about money.
- List ten beliefs you have about rich people.
- List ten beliefs you have about managing money.
- Notice the negative beliefs. Change them into positive ones and consciously change your thinking.
- Decide whether you want to forgive money, rich people in general or your parents, to move you through your financial-lack pattern.
- Do a Forgiveness Process on whichever feels the most negative to you.

I am safe. I am innocent. I am loved.

Just Breathe

my cat Cezanne

Trusting The Flowing Process of Life

In this moment
I feel grateful for all the good in my life.
I am grateful for the eyes to see this good,
no longer focusing on what is wrong in my life,
but focusing on what is happening
right in my life.
I know that when I do this more good happens to me
and becomes like a river
flowing endlessly from me out to the world.
I share this good with the world
and the world shares its good with me.
I am safe
and I am grateful.

– Juliana Ericson

> "I am not what happened to me. I am what I
> choose to become."   ~ Carl Jung

CHAPTER 16

The Journey Keeps Goin' On

> *"Many embark on a destination.*
> *Few realize it is the journey itself."*

Journal entry:

There is a brass plaque etched with this wisdom on a bench in Victoria, British Columbia. Sitting here overlooking this fabulous harbor, I am smelling the seaweed, hearing seagulls and enjoying the cool breeze. I absorb the words written here and am reminded of my own wonderful journey, my own enlivening process.

I began my quest for enlightenment at the age of sixteen. As I watched "The Graduate" I experienced my first break from conformity. The movie finished and I sat there without moving. I had to see it again. The main character, Benjamin Braddock, chose his own path, different from what his parents and peers expected from him. "What is this feeling?" I questioned myself. It was the moment of the beginning of my life's journey.

For many years to follow, I thought enlightenment was a destination. I assumed if I found the right method, did the right deed, followed the right person's teachings, learned the right information, and found the right key ... I would suddenly become enlightened. My intention was to find all of this before my fortieth birthday, so I could spend as much time in bliss as possible before moving on. (I chuckle now as I write this, realizing that my enlightenment did jump to hyperspeed at the age of 41. It wasn't an esoteric secret from a wise, old sage. I actually gained the most profound impetus from a lying lover. Gurus come in many shapes, sizes and forms!)

After many years of practicing this conscious breathing and deep emotional work, I am clear that life is a beautiful process of unfolding to our true nature. I no longer look to a time when I will be more peaceful. I am at peace now. I enjoy life's ebb and flow as I move in and out of peacefulness, aware that I am always at choice. I no longer look to a time when I will have everything I need to be happy. I have all I need now. I can decide to be happy in any moment. I no longer look to some future enlightenment when I'll have everything all figured out. I enjoy the fascinating moments of my life's unfolding now. I am enjoying the synchronicities and hidden magic in everyday life. I am delighted and fascinated to see what my mind creates, understanding that my outer world is constantly reflecting my inner thoughts and beliefs.

As I write this, I see a large group of Canadian geese slowly swimming by, reminding me of a new life lesson I learned last week. Geese have a leader when they fly, partly to organize their group, partly to create a wind flow that makes it easier for the followers to fly. As each goose in the "vee" flaps its wings, it creates an "uplift" for the birds that follow, and the whole flock adds a more than 70 percent greater flying range than if they flew alone. In exchange, the group constantly honks to encourage the leader, making his task lighter. Canadian geese have always been a model of teamwork for me.

Although the goose model is one I admire, I haven't always adhered to it. Because of that, I got into some hot water a couple of weeks ago. It began when I arranged with a colleague to conduct a workshop in Seattle, Washington, where she lived. It would be the week following my trip here to British Columbia. Cara had asked me a couple of times in the last year to lead a workshop in Seattle, and she was excited about the idea of organizing the workshop for me. I was also pleased about the arrangement, because I would earn enough from the workshop to pay for my entire vacation, which made me really happy. Three months was plenty of time for Cara to get the word out and create enrollment energy.

I had checked in with her four or five times and she would always say, "it's gonna be great!" Cara seemed pumped about the workshop, where she would be entitled half of the profits. She had organized workshops before and knew what to do, so I left it in her hands. Then, two days before I left for my trip, she emailed me and said she was sorry but could not organize the workshop. She had not signed anyone up, and she wanted to go to California with a friend instead.

I admit to being human with human feelings; I was shocked and disappointed… and angry. How could she? Where was honor and integrity in all of this? I wondered if I should cancel the workshop, or try to scramble and do whatever I could to create enough participants to continue? As I was packing and planning for my four-week trip, leaving in two days, I now had anger added to my pre-vacation emotional soup.

I gave myself a few hours to think about my options, then I knew what to do next. I could not function, I could NOT be present, I could not experience my wonderful upcoming vacation trip … unless I forgave Cara. The only way for me to be present was to do the Forgiveness Process on her. I began it that same day.

By Day Four, it was clear to me why I had co-created this experience: Canadian geese. The geese honk to encourage the leader on, but I had not done that with Cara. I was aware of her challenge at staying focused and her tendency to leave projects incomplete, because of her cesarean birth. Some support, as in weekly phone meetings to compare updates, would have helped her. Monthly goals, with me providing bi-weekly promo videos and other support tools, might have "honked" her back on the right track. What I had done instead was to leave it all on her plate. So, concurrently, I'm learning more about the importance of teamwork.

I am noticing an old pattern emerging in myself as I do this Forgiveness Process. I used to be all-or-nothing with about every aspect of my life. Over time, I've learned that balance is a more peaceful and empowered way to live, so I have reversed most of that pattern. I see there is one part I've held onto: I generally do things either completely on my own, or I hand it entirely over to others; there's no in-between, no teamwork. As a single woman for more than 20 years, I'm used to doing things on my own. Teamwork is helping each other succeed for the good of the whole. This workshop would have benefited the whole by enriching the lives of the anticipated large group of participants, as well as by financially helping both Cara and me.

I learned some valuable lessons with this process. I am reminded that enlightenment is never "done." It's a constant process of unearthing ourselves if we are open to learning a new way of being. I discovered that on a team I am more than I can be on my own. I am also reminded to trust the process of life while still trusting my journey.

ACTION: What patterns are you holding on to that no longer serve you? Imagine what your life would be like without those restricting patterns.

You are safe. You are innocent. You are loved.

by Nila Frederiksen

Being Peace

Today
I choose to let go of my small thinking.
I choose to step into the truth of who I really AM:
* a Divine Being created by Divinity.*
Remembering this I can make choices
* based on peace and brotherhood,*
*   instead of fear and separation.*
I want to live in peace with my worldly brothers and sisters.
I will do all I can today to make that happen.

– Juliana Ericson

"Forgiveness is not an occasional act, it is a constant attitude."

- Martin Luther King, Jr.

CHAPTER 17
The Role of Gratitude

I like to sit each morning on my garden patio filled with pots of colorful flowers, encased in a myriad of evergreens and flowering bushes. I start my days there reading a spiritually uplifting book, often *A Course in Miracles*, as I enjoy my morning coffee. Quietly I watch the birds eat, from my feeders or the berries planted around my patio. A variety of songbirds sing their beautiful morning music to me while the cicadas sing their low, steady chant in the background. It is still and solid and nurturing to my soul. Today is no different. The air is enveloped with the crispness of autumn. Leaves from my sycamore tree above me are beginning to drop its leaves onto my breakfast table and patio. Shadows are getting longer.

The stillness of this 8:00 Sunday morning is stunning. It's as if I'm in some ancient sacred temple; this natural stillness creates an atmosphere where I'm transported into an experience of awe and gratitude for this Divine presence I see and the Divine Love I feel. Now, as so often before, I feel as though my heart will burst out of my chest, unable to contain all of this Magnificent Love. Sobbing with tears, my body vibrates alive and I am aware of only all the goodness in my life and all around me. The bad seems to melt away into nonexistence. Only good and peace exist in these moments, my precious intimate communion with Holiness.

The grace of this awesome feeling is a Holy gift, and I am only able to receive it when it comes to me on its own. I've tried to make it happen, but cannot. There is one undercurrent in these moments of communion that is of my creation: I consciously push away the clumsiness of everyday life, allowing this graceful peace to fill my awareness. I then focus on the beauty around me and gratitude emerges. That gratitude opens the way for the ecstatic experience of Divine Presence within me. It is beyond mortal existence and beyond this world.

The reason I'm sharing this intimate experience with you here is that I have found over the years when I focus on the beauty or the good before me it almost always leads me to gratitude. When I focus on this high, I am not focusing on whatever bad is happening in my life at the time. I am allowing my body and mind to sink down into the core of my being, where I am safe and connected to my Source. No matter how wonderful we think our brains are, our feelings can only have one complete feeling at a time: love or fear, not both. I cannot feel fear when I am in this totally loving state I described. Conversely, when I am in a fearful state and begin to feel love, I am no longer in a totally fearful state. They cannot co-exist.

Fear is the great separator

After entering into this heavenly state, I am aware of my Divine connection to all things. When I am here, it's easier to see my part in a disagreement, or I'm able to better understand why someone made me angry. It's so much easier to see these things when I have removed myself from the perspective that made me angry in the first place, usually fear. Fear is beneath all anger. And fear is the "Great Separator": it separates us from others; it separates us from our joy and peace; it separates us from knowing God's unconditional Love and safety.

A state of gratitude, a state of being

Back to gratitude, I am a big believer in people trying their best to live in an ongoing state of gratitude. Gratitude makes all of life better, because we are focusing on the glass being half-full instead of half-empty, so to speak. It drastically brightens up all of our experiences, helping us live in a more positive way. As we make gratitude more our everyday life, it will become easier to live with a gratitude-seeking vision of that life. When we are in a state of gratitude, we're in a state ready to receive Holy gifts and beautiful synchronicities. When we are in gratitude, our hearts are open, ready to give as well as receive. It creates a win/win situation.

You may have heard about the benefits of keeping a gratitude journal. This is a wonderful way to teach mind/body/spirit the value of the life-changing instrument of gratitude. When you list the things for which you are grateful, you are more likely to seek out other things for which to be grateful. It's along the lines of when you have a new roof installed on your house; you're more likely to notice other new roofs. Or, if you see a new wrinkle on your face, you are likely to find other new wrinkles also. You can also say that what you focus on expands. The main idea is to do what you can to stay in a state of gratitude and appreciation. When you do this you will lift yourself out of this world and into the sacred, closer to your real home.

For years I have included gratitude as an integral part of my daily spiritual practice. In my morning prayer I ask that God use me as an instrument of peace and healing, confident that as I surrender I am held in the arms of Love. In the evening it's like opening a bunch of surprise gifts, as I look back at my day with gratitude. I see the times, small and large, when Holy Presence has used me to help someone or myself. (The tiny ones are often my favorites, because in the moment they seem so insignificant.) But looking back at my day with the higher perspective of knowing God is in charge, I see that even the tiny miracles are important. It gives me a sense of purpose knowing that I've surrendered my day and it was worthy of being used by Divine Intervention. God can use anything for His purposes, and when I surrendered my day, it was worthy. It was given as a gift to God, then through the door of gratitude the gift was reciprocated. You may have similar experiences.

Yes, gratitude is powerful when used in this way to punctuate my days. It's even more powerful when used on a consistent, low-keyed basis beneath all you do and say. Being grateful to someone who angers me after they cut me off in traffic can be quite a spiritual moment! Why use gratitude then? I can be grateful to the anger for showing me I have someone or something to forgive that is still lingering in my innermost thoughts. Is it fear of losing control? Maybe it's a former lover, maybe it's my father, maybe it's an ex-friend. Maybe I need to forgive myself. All I know is that I look to the thought beneath the anger. We are never upset for the reason we think we are, it's always something else. We can use those anger thoughts as tools to clear out our minds and bodies to help us live freer and happier lives. All the while, our healing is helping to heal the world.

As a footnote, I received a phone call today from my good friend, Barbara, thanking me for having her over yesterday for treats and conversation on my patio. I so appreciated her gratitude. It felt good for my loving gift to my wonderful friend to be received. I am grateful for all things, big and small.

ACTION: List ten things in this moment for which you are grateful. Try to do this for one week.

You are safe. You are innocent. You are loved.

by Nila Frederiksen

Looking for the Good

Today I will stop my mind
> *each time I recognize it is judging, blaming*
>> *or looking at a negative version*
>> *of what I am seeing.*
I realize I have been addicted to seeing only the bad in situations.
I have not given myself a chance
> *to see a positive version of the same experience.*
Today, even if I don't see the situation
> *as a complete reversed version*
I will still look for bits of good there.
> *The more I do this*
>> *the more I will create a positive worldview*
>> *in which to live.*
I prefer to live in peace and harmony.
I will look for the good today.

– Juliana Ericson

"We must develop and maintain the capacity to forgive. He who is devoid of the power to forgive is devoid of the power to love. There is some good in the worst of us and some evil in the best of us. When we discover this, we are less prone to hate our enemies."

- Martin Luther King, Jr

CHAPTER 18
Some Anger Management Ideas

The world we see is a reflection of our thoughts, and is usually a fearful self-image. Look instead on the world with charity and love and see how your world will change. *"Be the change you want to see in the world."* Mahatma Gandhi said. What he was saying is that we must change our minds and our actions if we want our world to change. We cannot expect the fear-based world to change first, before we change. That type of thinking is what has gone on for thousands of years. Anger has led to attack, which has led to revenge, which has led to anger, attack, and so on. It is a vicious cycle that has not worked. Revenge and hatred have ruled our societies for millennia, and we are no more civilized now than we were at the beginning. Society has continued to pick up a gun before considering compassionate listening as a pathway to peace.

A standard phrase I use with my clients is: "You are not doing this Forgiveness Process only for yourself. You are also doing it for your family and friends. Your forgiveness work is going to affect the whole world. Everything is connected, so when you change, everything changes."

I liken it to a large bowl full of ping pong balls. Picture this clear bowl of balls with a string attached to the bottom ball. What happens when you pull that bottom ping pong ball out of the bowl? Every ball shifts to fill the spot where the bottom ball had been. Every ball is affected by the shift of that one ball that was once at the bottom, but has changed as it was lifted up.

This is exactly what happens with us when we make a shift, good or bad. This shift is powerful to all those around us when we release an old hate. How much positive energy do you think is released into the world when we forgive and no longer hate? It is a massively gigantic amount! (This theory is sometimes referred to as The *Butterfly Effect*: the phenomenon whereby a small change at one place in a complex system can have large effects elsewhere. For example, a butterfly flapping its wings in Rio de Janeiro might change the weather in Chicago. (*Source*: The Farlex Free Dictionary).

> *"There is nothing your holiness cannot do. Your holiness reverses all the laws of the world. It is beyond every restriction of time, space, distance and limits of any kind. Your holiness is totally*

> *unlimited in its power because it establishes you*
> *as a (Child) of God, at one with the Mind of his*
> *Creator. There is nothing your holiness cannot do*
> *because the power of God lies in it."*
> *- A Course in Miracles,* Workbook lesson 38

An experiment for you

Allow your anger to subside for a few minutes. In your mind's eye, I want you to offer compassion to the person with whom you're angry, having problems, difficulties or suffering. Allow your holiness to speak for you. Pretend you are that person with whom you are angry. Speak from their perspective about why they did what they did to you. What was going on in her life? What fear was he experiencing? Spend a few minutes in this emotionally stretching exercise before you finish. Even if you aren't completely reversed in your negative thinking about that person with whom you are angry, you will certainly be a few steps closer to some peace. Give yourself praise for even attempting this exercise. I thank you.

I am aware that all of this might seem too big a stretch for you. I know there are some things people experience that are too horrific to even comprehend. But it's still a choice for them to live in hate or not, to live in hell or not. (I'm saying "hell" because of the loveless and lonely meaning it has to most people.) The fact is that often when I mention Forgiveness, usually what people ask first is, "But how are we supposed to forgive horrible offenses like murder?" Our fear-based ego-mind will go immediately to the extreme, trying to prove its case. It bases its protective prison on fear and, like a good lawyer, will try to find any loophole in the case of compassion that it can. Think of change in small increments and it's easier to comprehend. We can make changes one small choice at a time. Life truly is what we make of it, and we make it with the thoughts we choose. Choose anger and separation, and that's the life you will experience. Choose compassion and acceptance, and those will be in your life.

Is it you or is it others?

I know a woman who is always complaining about how mean people are to her, how angry she is because she's often being disrespected. I have seen it to be true. People who've known her for years have stopped asking her to parties, stopped visiting her, and discontinued friendly conversation. She's been dropped from jobs for no apparent reason. She has a terrible relationship with her daughter because they're constantly fighting. She's the one who usually gets the wrong dinner from the waitress, and she will have to complain to the manager. She's the one with so many physical pains, which give her even more to complain about.

What I have noticed is that as this woman is complaining about others disrespecting her, I hear her speak with such a condescending tone to them, or with anger bubbling beneath her words. It's as though she is asking for or expecting a fight. You might think that her actions are a result of her mistreatments, but I suggest that her mistreatments stem from her actions. I believe she made a subconscious decision years ago that people were out to get her, for whatever reason, and she is constantly living out her reactivity to that belief. She is creating her hell with a choice that life is not safe. Her hell is that she is separated from friends and jobs and children. She's not a victim; she has created this life with her own thoughts.

Pain cannot live in the present. Can you imagine how her life could be, if she stopped living in the past where her original hurt was? She could be changed if she'd see the waitress as merely an innocent bystander in her life. She'd be different if she could be grateful to the daughter who bore the granddaughter she so adores. If this woman would be grateful for the good she found in her life, focusing on that instead of on her painful past, she might find that the pain in her body could possibly be a result of holding on to that past. We all have freedom of choice, no matter what country in which we live.

What to do when you are angered

When you feel angered by someone, try these three steps I learned from listening to Rev. Ed Bacon, during an insightful interview with Oprah Winfrey on the OWN Network:

One: Stop and take a breath before you respond.
Two: Step back to observe what is happening (a few seconds, minutes, hours, days; in extreme cases, even months).

Three: Is there a higher response that will allow you to keep your power? (That Is, is there another way of looking at this that will allow me not to be as angered?)

It's helpful to have a plan to use for when you know you generally fail at something. When you know you're going to a fabulous party and are on a diet, it helps to eat some low-fat food before you leave, so you won't be tempted to fill up on the high-fat party food. If you're at a wedding celebration where they are serving a fine French champagne you adore, it helps to drink every other glass as sparkling water so you won't become inebriated. If you know you get angered by a particular situation or person, it helps to have a talk with yourself ahead of time. Practice these three steps ahead of time, so you will remember them in the moment of a possible confrontation.

Pray. I have found that when I ask God to be there with me, to speak through me, I'm more likely to have a positive outcome. I remember when my then-13-year-old son and I were disagreeing about an issue. It was becoming really heated and evident that neither of us was going to back down. I excused myself to the other room and said a quick prayer, asking Spirit to be present in our argument. When I returned to the room, the phone rang. It was a wrong number, but the person said something so ridiculous that we both burst out laughing. It broke our anger and we came to a settlement. See, things don't always have to be so difficult. Sometimes God's sense of humor is surprising!

Three common causes of anger

The three common sources of anger are guilt, blame and shame. If these insidious emotions are left unattended for long, they usually morph into anger and resentment. The origins of these real or imagined hurts are in the past, often far back into the past. When we hold onto these hurts our heart responds by shutting down emotionally, preventing us from enjoying love in the present. Holding blame for someone who hurt us years ago creates a prison to live in, and keeps us from recognizing that we hold our own key to freedom.

When we adapt to living with these burdens of anger and resentment, we close ourselves down. We expect to experience pain again, so we live in constant defense and fear. The longer we live with this pattern, the more we continue to unconsciously create evidence that it's true. We continue to create emotional pain for ourselves, and reasons to blame people. Let's stop that cycle of self-flagellation.

Blaming others for something you feel they said or did wrong to you is a way of making yourself the victim. You are simply handing them permission to have power over you. They will follow your victim-thinking direction by NOT being kind or sorry, or making any other change a compassionate person would. You may say you want them to change and be nice to you, but of course they will not. They won't, because they are reacting to the subconscious programmed expectations that you've "taught" them. You expect them to be mean, and so they will be mean.

Another victim-thinking way to look at blame is

that we blame others for how badly we feel. We cannot imagine we've caused such pain and suffering to ourselves. You will stay as the victim until you decide to choose differently.

Guilt and shame

The other two common sources of anger are guilt and shame. These we create to remind us of all the countless times we've hurt others. Guilt and shame cause self-blame making us feel helpless, as does blame. Common core thoughts that can originate from these debilitating subconscious feelings are, *I'm bad, I'm not worthy, I can't, I hurt people, I'm guilty.* These thoughts are lies and must be transformed!

Guilt is not the same as remorse. There is an activity in the feeling of remorse, a "mustard seed" of willingness to change. In remorse, there's a kind of sadness for what we may have done wrong and we're inspired to improve our past mistakes and failings.

Guilt is a form of punishment, but to ourselves. Guilt has a tendency to paralyze us to move forward with positive change. It is possible to let go of worthless feelings of guilt and create a positive remorse. We can say, "I have messed up for the last time. I see why I used to make these mistakes, but now I have learned how to think differently. I can choose another way, and I want to make my life better." It's usually easier to move out of that negative direction if there is a powerful reason to change, such as the love of children,

If you have a long standing pattern of anger, consider some of the anger-management programs available. These therapies often come within the schools of CBT (Cognitive Behavioral Therapies) and in modern systems such as REBT (Rational Emotive Behavior Therapy). The insights and tools you will receive there will be of great value to you and to your relationships. Anger-management programs work for some people, even before doing the Forgiveness Processes, to get beyond anger.

It can be difficult to see any possibility of joy or peace when you are still angry with someone and are not willing to move past it. You might need a little extra help. We've all been hurt by others in some way and have conversely retaliated. We hurt others in defense of our hurt, as do others. It can be a great life lesson for us to learn that all of us as humans are hurting in some way inside.

Cognitive behavioral affective therapy

One new integrative approach to anger treatment has been formulated by Ephrem Fernandez. It has been created as a new integrative approach to anger treatment. Called CBAT (cognitive behavioral affective therapy), this treatment teaches people how to deal with the onset, progression and residual effects of their anger. CBAT uses relaxation and reappraisal in addition to cognitive and behavioral systems, adding beneficial techniques for people to use while they are actually feeling the anger rising within them.

Heart coherence training

A new approach I'm especially excited about is heart coherence training. It shows us how our hearts and minds can communicate, to make huge improvements easily in mind and body. An anger study of 3129 participants shows that 50 percent of their anger decreased by the end of the training. This approach uses biofeedback and specially created mindfulness techniques. Heart Coherence Training actually produces a positive shift in their heart rhythm, stabilizing the autonomic nervous system. This is especially important because this technique will reduce the stress-hormone cortisol, known for being a significant cause of heart problems.

This technique is also known to raise the levels of the "feel-good" hormone, DHEA. In addition, the negative effects on the immune system that anger causes can be reversed when people use the heart coherence methods. Bruce Wilson, MD, Chairman, Heart Hospital of Milwaukee, gives his opinion on heart coherence and similar processes: "These tools are effective in breaking the cycle of anger and all of its consequences, are extremely easy to learn and are based on elegant scientific research that has taught, and also shown us, [that] the heart and the brain communicate."

ACTION: Focus on your heart. Take ten long, slow breaths in and through your heart. Feel the peace you create.

You are safe. You are innocent. You are loved.

"My Meditation Place" by Juliana Ericson
www.JulianaNashville.com

The Whole World Says Yes to Me

My eyes are opened
      because of my new forgiving nature.
I see a world that loves me more than I knew.
I feel the warm presence of caring and concern
      I had not noticed before.
My heart, too, feels as though it is melting open,
      blending with the loving world around me.
Although this life has been here in plain sight,
I am only now recognizing its beauty
      and I receive it with my opened arms.

– Juliana Ericson

*"Forgiveness is the fragrance the violet sheds
on the heel that has crushed it."*

- Mark Twain

CHAPTER 19

*Creating Your Own
Garden of Forgiveness*

Gardens have a way of nurturing our bodies and souls. They are places for us to be transformed, absorbing nature's healing balm when we may not find it anywhere else. Being in nature is one of the most healing things we can do for our bodies. Its beauty and color brings us solace through our eyes. Fragrances can heal us through our powerful olfactory systems with scents of nature such as lavender, lilac and gardenia. The plants produce oxygen which nourishes us physically. A garden provides us with a sense of innocence and peace, nourishing our emotions in a unique way. These special places in nature can gently nudge us to begin our journeys of reconciliation and forgiveness.

You can create your own special place to support your forgiveness work. I call these "Forgiveness Gardens." These gardens can openly show our belief in the power of forgiveness as a tool for healing and transformation of conflict. Although they are not necessary for you to work on your Forgiveness Process, they will infinitely inspire you to continue your process of compassionate tolerance and change. They can support you, by providing a sacred space in which to release your anger, to weep and to let go of the emotional pain. It's also an intimate place where you may choose to burn your anger letter, Part One in the process. Forgiveness Gardens provide solace and innocence as you write your seven days of letting-go statements, Part Two of the Forgiveness Process. They are also there to hold you up and give you courage in Part Three, as you write the final completion letter. Forgiveness Gardens support us with Love and Nature as we heal and move past suffering to our higher natures and the peace beyond.

The elements

As in any garden the basic structure is important. I like to use these components:

- a bench
- a focus, maybe spiritual in nature (suggestions below)
- a hard surface, such as a plastic clipboard, to write upon

- a plastic box to keep pen, paper & a lighter dry
- a burning bowl
- a fire pit
- kindling and small logs, covered to stay dry
- a lounge chair, hammock or reclining place
- a bird feeder
- a fountain, with plug or solar version
- a light or lantern
- a patio umbrella or painted tarp to be stretched (optional)
- some bushes, flowers and one or more trees

If at all possible, create this garden in a private place, the quieter, the better. If you cannot keep the outside noise down, use a fountain that can help neutralize the noise with its soothing water sounds. Be sure you place your burning bowl or fire pit on a non-flammable surface. You may have sparks of anger coming out from inside you, but you don't want any real sparks causing fires.

If you have a tree in your yard, that might be a first possibility for your Forgiveness Garden location. Trees are gentle and nourishing while giving lovely shade and coolness. An added plus is that their leaves absorb surrounding noises. Just make sure your fire pit is outside the branch area.

Try placing the bench with your back to the house and people, planting bushes behind the bench. This is a very intimate and personal process to be done in safety and seclusion, which the bushes help create. It's nurturing to have bushes or trees that move in the wind and provide gentle movement, signifying how a happy life requires us to move and bend with life's changes. It's also a good idea to have some evergreen bushes, so your garden has structure to enjoy all year round. You might place a hammock or lounge chair in your garden to create a place for safe contemplation.

It is essential to *feel* the design of this garden. Don't just consider what it looks like. The main purpose of this garden is to support and nurture you through a challenging emotional process, so feeling the design is of utmost importance. Your Forgiveness Garden need not be large, but it does need to change the way you feel when you enter it. That is your measure of success. How does it make you feel as you enter?

The most important element of this garden is that it provides solace for you, the user. Another important element is a focal point or points. These could be spiritual in nature, such as a statue of St. Francis of Assisi, Martin Luther King Jr., Jesus, Buddha, Mary, Gandhi, a Goddess figure or a Peace Pole. Your focal point could also be an inspiring quote etched onto a brass plate nailed to a wooden post, such as "Do I want to be right or happy?" or "Forgiveness simply means to let go." You could add a pond for reflecting, or for tossing stones of resentment into as you watch the ripples dissolve. How about a Zen sand focal point to use as you contemplate, moving a wooden stick through a sandbox as you consider your avenues of forgiveness? Or simply a rock or two, with words painted on them like "Peace" or "Forgive."

You could plant flowers in the ground or place pots of flowers in your garden. Plant fragrant flowers in pastel, soothing colors near your resting place. Nurture your senses! Either works fine, although potted plants usually require more watering than in-ground planted ones do. If you only have a hard surface available to you, try laying down outdoor carpet or artificial turf over the concrete in your garden area. In a sunny area you can add a patio umbrella, maybe one sewn with artificial flowers. Or, try a canvas tarp, roller-painted with pastel colors of pink and gold, in abstract blotches stretched across the area by wire from poles stuck in the ground.

Bird feeders bring life and innocence to your garden. The fountain brings momentum, neutralizes noise and reminds us that life is an ever-flowing river of wondrous experiences. A solar fountain is a good option for those without a power outlet nearby. Wind chimes offer beautiful, comforting melodies as they blow in the wind. Wind flags, written with supportive words and phrases such as "love" or "let it go," and ribbons that blow with the breezes are another option for beautiful movement in your garden.

After burning your angry letter in your burning bowl or fire pit, sprinkle the ashes on your garden flowers. The poisonous words have alchemized into nutrients for your life and your garden. Trust the ever-nurturing process of life!

Flower suggestions & their meanings

Here are some suggestions for flowers to use that have special significance. Use only soft-edged leaves in your garden; no cacti. (Flower ideas here are from the Campaign for Love and Forgiveness website.)

Flowers

Baby's Breath: everlasting love

Chrysanthemums: long life, prosperity, contemplation

Coneflower: life, conviviality

Forget-Me-Not: true love

Gardenia: transport of joy, ecstasy

Heather: solitude

Honeysuckle: generosity

Lily: purity, majesty

Orchid: perfection

Pansy: thoughtfulness

Peonies: love, marriage, fertility

Rose: love in all its forms

Sedum: tranquility

Sunflowers: sacred

Vines: regeneration

Water Lilies: purity, truth

Trees

Olive: forgiveness, peace

Flowering Almond: hope

Bamboo: loyalty, steadfastness

Birch: grace

Bodhi Tree: enlightenment

Cedar: strength

Cherry: spring, youth

Dogwood: love undiminished by adversity, durability

Hawthorn: hope

Magnolias: beauty, gentleness

Peach: immortality

Lilac: first love

Yew: faith, rebirth

Herbs

    Chamomile: energy in adversity, patience, wisdom
    Chervil: sincerity
    Dill: preservation, good spirits
    Fennel: worthy of all praise, strength
    Lavender: loyalty
    Lemon Verbena: enchantment
    Marjoram: joy, happiness
    Mint: eternal refreshment, wisdom, virtue
    Oregano: joy, happiness
    Parsley: useful knowledge, feast, joy, victory
    Rosemary: remembrance, love, loyalty, fidelity
    Sage: wisdom, long life, esteem, immortality
    Thyme: courage, strength

Oleander was the first plant to grow in the bombed and devastated area of Nagasaki and Hiroshima at the end of World War II. Although they are poisonous if ingested by humans and animals, they are a beautiful and meaningful plant to add to a tropical Forgiveness Garden.

These are just suggestions for you to inspire you to create your garden. Take charge yourself and be sure to check on whether you or your animals are allergic to any of these plants before planting them in your garden.

A few books to inspire you in planning your garden

Spiritual Gardening, by Peg Streep. This book is one of my very favorite spiritual gardening books. It has beautiful photographs and illustrations as well as rich resources for ways to help you connect your spirit to nature as you engage your senses. Your small urban plots or larger country spaces can become places to foster personal growth and spiritual awareness. Spiritual Gardening will inspire you with pictures of a broad range of gardens including tranquility, *feng shui*, aromatherapy, and labyrinths. There is even a chapter on gardening as a spiritual exercise.

Cultivating Sacred Space: Gardening for the Spirit, by Elizabeth Murray is another one full of inspiration and resources. Murray, a garden designer, has divided the book into four sections for each of the four seasons, with design elements for each. I have used this book over and over again for various sacred garden planning, small and large.

Gardens of the Spirit, by Roni Jay. This book includes pictures and descriptions of different types of gardens, including Zen, Islamic and Healing Gardens.

The Inward Garden: Creating a Place of Beauty and Meaning, by Julie Moir Mosservy, has information and beautiful photographs illustrating what I am suggesting when I say "How does your garden feel when you enter?" Gardens in these photographs feel sacred and intimate.

ACTION: Establish a special place where you can go to do your Forgiveness work now:
- a special chair next to a lighted candle;
- a bench outside with a pot of lovely flowers beside it; or
- a large cushion on the floor with a beautiful prayer rug underneath.

Plan a simple Forgiveness Garden for yourself, if you are so inclined.

You are safe. You are innocent. You are loved.

"I Am Wanted" by Juliana Ericson
www.JulianaNashville.com

My Love Is Important

Today
I will practice an exercise in holiness.
I will extend goodness to each person
 who enters my mind today.
Every person I greet I will inwardly bless.
I understand
 that as I do these things
  I am affecting the entire world,
   knowing that even minor acts of kindness
    are important parts of the whole.

– Juliana Ericson

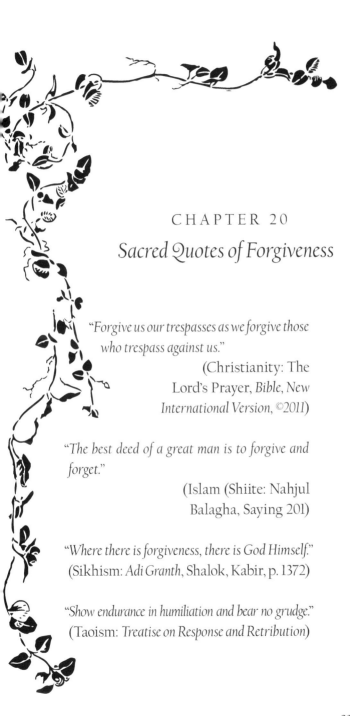

CHAPTER 20

Sacred Quotes of Forgiveness

"Forgive us our trespasses as we forgive those who trespass against us."

(Christianity: The Lord's Prayer, *Bible, New International Version,* ©2011)

"The best deed of a great man is to forgive and forget."

(Islam (Shiite: Nahjul Balagha, Saying 201)

"Where there is forgiveness, there is God Himself."
(Sikhism: *Adi Granth*, Shalok, Kabir, p. 1372)

"Show endurance in humiliation and bear no grudge."
(Taoism: *Treatise on Response and Retribution*)

"If you efface and overlook and forgive, then lo! God is forgiving, merciful." (Islam: *Qur'an* 64.14)

"The superior man tends to forgive wrongs and deals leniently with crimes."
(Confucianism: *I Ching* 40: Release)

"… [I]f you are offering your gift at the altar and there remember that your brother or sister has something against you, leave your gift there in front of the altar. First go and be reconciled to them; then come and offer your gift."
(Christianity: *Matthew* 5.23-24, *Bible, New International Version,* ©2011)

"The Day of Atonement atones for sins against God, not for sins against man, unless the injured person has been appeased."
(Judaism: *Mishnah,* Yoma 8.9)

"You shall not take vengeance or bear any grudge against the sons of your own people, but you shall love your neighbor as yourself: I am the Lord."
(Judaism and Christianity: *Leviticus* 19.18, *Bible, Revised Standard Version*)

"Who takes vengeance or bears a grudge acts like one who, having cut one hand while handling a knife, avenges himself by stabbing the other hand."
(Judaism: *Jerusalem Talmud,* Nedarim 9.4)

"Moses son of Imran said, 'My Lord, who is the
greatest of Thy servants in Thy estimation?' and
received the reply, 'The one who forgives when he
is in a position of power.'"

(Islam: *Hadith of Baihaqi*)

"Then Peter came up and said to him, 'Lord,
how often shall my brother sin against me, and
I forgive him? As many as seven times?' Jesus
said to him, 'I do not say to you seven times, but
seventy times seven.' "

(Christianity: *Bible, Revised Standard Version*)

(When Jesus was crucified, Roman
soldiers pierced him and Jesus prayed for
his enemies): "*Father, forgive them; for they
know not what they do....*"

(Christianity: *Luke 23:34, Bible,
English Standard Version*, ©2001)

"Even at the moment of death on the cross, Jesus
was so earnest in forgiving. His very last act was
motivated by his love for his enemies. He was the
supreme form of giving—a paragon of love. The
example of Jesus Christ is the absolute standard
for all mankind. Just imagine an entire nation
composed of Jesus-like men. What would you call
it? The Kingdom of Heaven on earth—it could be
nothing less."

- Unification Church:
Sun Myung Moon, 10- 20-73

"You cannot truly forgive yourself or others as long as you derive your sense of self from the past. Only by accessing the power of the Now, which is your own power, can there be true forgiveness. This renders the past powerless, and you realize deeply that nothing you ever did or that was ever done to you could touch even in the slightest the radiant essence of who you are. The whole concept of forgiveness then becomes unnecessary."

‐ Eckhart Tolle, *The Power of Now*

"Sacred Feminine" by Juliana Ericson
www.JulianaNashville.com

With Help, I Can Do It

Today if I begin to feel angered
I will remember the three ways I can use
    to avoid becoming incensed:
        breathe,
            observe
                and imagine.
When I feel angered
I will stop and take a few long, slow breaths.
I will then observe what is happening
    from a third-party perspective.
After that I will imagine what other way could I respond
    that would keep my power
        and keep my peace.
I always know I can call on my friend and guide, God,
    to show me a solution.
I am confident I am never alone.

– Juliana Ericson

> "Darkness cannot drive out darkness: only light can do that. Hate cannot drive out hate: only love can do that."
>
> — Martin Luther King, Jr.

CHAPTER 21

Support Sources, Traditional & Not

Sometimes it helps to get some support when doing your Forgiveness Process. You may need help to get inspired or to get through an especially difficult time. Here are a few suggestions:

Digital help, videos and websites:

Watch this amazing video for some raw and heartfelt inspiration. The man in this video forgives his brother's murderer face to face. I am moved every time I watch it. http://youtube/P0hgglAN2s4

Ho'Oponopono is a Hawaiian Forgiveness Process which I have found to be very helpful in moving clients to a state of willingness to forgive. Here is a five-minute meditation that uses the breath prayer: "I am sorry. Please forgive me. I love you. Thank you." You can also do this prayer anytime you feel upset with a person. http://is.gd/zQQJwj

Try just getting it off your chest! Here is a website where you can write a card to someone *anonymously* and post it for the world to see. Sometimes just saying out loud a deep seated anger that's been stuffed and hidden can release it. What I like about this website is that it makes known to thousands of people what you're angry about, although no one can tell who you are or to whom you are referring. (http://www.postsecret.com/)

The Forgiveness Project uses storytelling to help people see how forgiveness, reconciliation and conflict resolution can create positive changes in victims and perpetrators. They provide tools to promote behavioral change, reversing revenge and retaliation. They share evidence that Forgiveness can heal individuals, communities and even entire nations (http://theforgivenessproject.com)

A Campaign for Forgiveness Research is a place to learn about scientific research on the subject of forgiveness. "Forgiveness that is offered, received, or observed can bring the power of forgiveness into your own world," they propose. www.forgiving.org

The Peace Alliance empowers civic engagement toward a culture of peace. They are an alliance of advocates of peace-building from throughout the United States. Their work is mainly to take peace-building from the margins of societal discourse to policy priorities. They have hundreds of volunteer teams throughout the U.S. including cities, colleges and high schools. www.thepeacealliance.org

Rasur Foundation (http:/www.rasurfoundation. org/) offers a practice that combines a scientifically proven method for "feeling peace" with a clear path for "speaking peace" that creates authentic, compassionate connection.

Be Peace is an online community bulletin board of inspiring art, music, stories, and writings contributed by anyone who would like to share. (www.bepeace.org)

Heart Math. The Institute of HeartMath is an internationally recognized nonprofit research and education organization, dedicated to helping people reduce stress, self-regulate emotions and build energy and resilience for healthy, happy lives. HeartMath tools, technology and training teach people to rely on the intelligence of their hearts in concert with their minds at home, school, work and play. (http://www.heartmath.org)

The Culture of Peace Initiative (CPI) is a local and global Peace Building Initiative that aims at uniting their strengths along diverse pathways to a realized a culture of peace in the world. CPI highlights inter-cultural and inter-generational people who are sharing their version of peace building. (www.cultureofpeace.org)

The Center for Nonviolent Communication is an organization based on the principles of nonviolence: the state of compassion when no violence is present in the heart, which they believe to be our natural state. Founded by Marshall Rosenberg, CNVC has found that people who practice NVC (non-violent communication) enjoy greater authenticity in their communication, have increased understanding and realize the importance of conflict resolution. "NVC assumes that we all share the same, basic human needs, and that each of our actions are a strategy to meet one or more of these needs," their website states. (www.cnvc.org)

Films For Peace (www.films4peace.org) is a forum of contemporary artists interpreting peace.

Some U.S. sources of Breathwork Practitioners:

www.breathworkers.com (Atlanta, Georgia);
www.newyorkrebirthingbreathwork.com
    (New York, New York);
http://www.philadelphiarebirthing.com
    (Philadelphia, Pennsylvania);
http://www.transformationsusa.com
    (Milwaukee, Wisconsin);
http://powerofbreath.com (Spofford, New Hampshire).

Aromatherapy:

I have found that aromatherapy is a beautiful and gentle way to calm me down when I'm anxious or overwhelmed. I feel it can also work for people who are doing the Forgiveness Process. Here are some examples for you to consider:

MYRRH has one of the highest levels of *sesquiterpenes*, a class of compounds that has direct effects on the hypothalamus, pituitary, and amygdala, which is the seat of our emotions. It is restorative and inspiring. Myrrh is known to be helpful for people who feel emotionally stuck and want to move forward in their lives. It is also used to support a state of grace.

A popular essential OIL BLEND "FORGIVENESS" by Young Living Essential Oils contains Frankincense, Sandalwood, Lavender, Melissa, Angelica, Helichrysum, Rose, Rosewood, Geranium, Lemon, Palmarosa, Ylang Ylang, Bergamot, Roman Chamomile, and Jasmine.

Another OIL BLEND is "RELEASE", also by Young Living Medical Grade Essential Oils. (http://www.youngliving.com)/ - use #1101051 or order directly through me at http://breathworks.net/

(These products are not intended to diagnose, treat, cure, or prevent any disease.)

Peace organizations *(from the Culture of Peace Initiative)*:

Earthdance International
ENO Programme
Friends of the United Nations
Gaia Field Project
IDP Vigils
Institute for Multi-Track Diplomacy
International Cities of Peace
Interpeace
MasterPeace
Mayors for Peace
MedMob
National Peace Academy
Odyssey Networks
PeaceJam

Peace In The Park

Peace One Day

Peace Pals International

Pinwheels for Peace

Playing for Change

Push4Peace

Roots and Shoots / Jane Goodall Institute

Service for Peace

The Global Alliance for Ministries & Infrastructures
for Peace

The Global Alliance for the Prevention of Armed Conflict

The Global Mala Project

The Global Peace Film Festival

The International Association of Peace Messenger Cities

The Peace Alliance

The Shift Network

Think Peace Network

United Religions Initiative

We The World

We Want Peace

ABOUT THE AUTHOR

Juliana Ericson has been a Life Enhancement Coach and a Conscious Breathwork Coach for 17 years. She teaches the power of forgiveness and explains how our personal core negative beliefs affect our lives. She teaches about birth and prenatal psychology, and how those experiences create our patterns as adults.

Juliana compassionately guides clients through gentle processes, such as circular breathing, freeing them from self-defeating thought patterns which might have begun before birth and during the birth process. She teaches Life Coaching and Breathwork schools, conducts workshops on a variety of life-enhancing subjects, is a Loving Relationships Facilitator in Training and maintains a private practice in Nashville, Tennessee.

Juliana also presents corporate talks about the power of Breathwork, including to Vanderbilt University's Nursing Midwives. Although she is an ordained elder with the Presbyterian Church USA, she is a seeker and uses her passion for the sacred from many other traditions, such as Sufi, Hindu, Native American and Buddhist. Juliana is also a professional artist, and paints in her home studio.

She recently published "Activate More Passion & Purpose in YOU!", a workbook with daily mind-expanding and heart-expanding exercises. For years people have questioned her about what she does to stay centered and excited about life. She was inspired to compile this easy-to-follow book with many of her favorite daily practices. It's available on Amazon.com (http://is.gd/F90yGF)

For in-person, phone or Skype sessions with Juliana, you may reach her through www.Breathworks.net. Follow her daily inspirational postings on her Facebook page: https://www.facebook.com/Breathetoheal

Juliana is also a professional, award-winning artist and paints in her studio located in Nashville, Tennessee. You can find her work at: www.JulianaNashville.com

Dear God, May my life be a divine expression
of our Love for each other. Amen